MAKE it WORK!

OLD JAPAN

Andrew Haslam & Clare Doran

Consultant: Heidi Potter, B.A.

A **TWO-CAN** BOOK
published by
THOMSON LEARNING

First published in Great Britain in 1995 by
Two-Can Publishing Ltd

First published in the United States in 1995 by
Thomson Learning
New York

Library of Congress Cataloging-in-Publication Data

Haslam, Andrew.
    Old Japan / Andrew Haslam.
        p.   cm. -- (Make it work! History)
    Includes index.
    Summary: Discusses how the Japanese, throughout history, developed
a way of life that sustained them both physically and spiritually.
Incudes projects such as making a kimono, paper, and sushi.
    ISBN 1-56847-139-4
    1. Japan--Social life and customs--Juvenile literature. 2. Japan-
-Social life and customs--Pictorial works--Juvenile literature.
[1. Japan--Social life and customs. 2. Handicraft.] I. Title.
II. Series.
    DS821.H3493 1995
    390'.0952--dc20   95-31536

Managing Editor: Christine Morley
Editor: Jacqueline McCann
Senior Designer: Helen McDonagh
Art Director: Jill Plank
Deputy Art Director: Carole Orbell
Research: Deborah Kespert
Picture Researcher: Dipika Palmer-Jenkins
Model-makers: Corina Holzherr, Paul Holzherr, Melanie Williams
Thanks to Tim at Westpoint Studio and Peter Davies

Models: Robert Blankson, Lester Cotier, Catherine Dawes, Anteneh Elcock, Matthew Guest, Amy Kwan, Ana Ivanovic,
Charlotte Walters, Miki Zoric.

Photographic credits: Ancient Art & Architecture Collection: p4 (bl), p41, p54; Chris Uhlenbeck: p9, p17, p33, p34; Helen
McDonagh: map p8; The Hulton-Deutsch Collection: p14; Japan Archive: p57; Japan National Tourist Office: p60; JICC:
p28; Michael Holford: p12, p27; Robert Harding Picture Library: p4 (tr); Tony Stone Worldwide: p46; Victoria & Albert
Museum: p40, p50; Werner Forman Archive: p26; Zefa Photo Library: p20, p24, p34, p38, p42, p58, p61.

All other photographs by Ray Moller
Printed and bound by G. Canale & C. SpA, Turin, Italy

2 4 6 8 10 9 7 5 3 1

Contents

Studying Japan's Past

All human beings need food and shelter to survive. They also need a system of beliefs to give shape and meaning to their lives. Throughout history, people have found different ways of meeting these basic needs. By studying the people of Japan, we learn how they developed a way of life that has sustained them, physically and spiritually.

IN THIS BOOK, we look at four different periods of Japanese history, each one telling us something new about the Japanese way of life and character. We know how people lived during these times through the writings and paintings that were made then and from the work of **historians**.

Each period is represented by a symbol that is used when information refers mainly to that time. Where there is no symbol, it means that the information generally applies to all four periods.

KEY FOR SYMBOLS

(fan) Heian 790–1185

(swords) Kamakura 1185–1333

(tea bowl) Muromachi and Momoyama 1392–1600

(woodcut) Edo 1600–1868

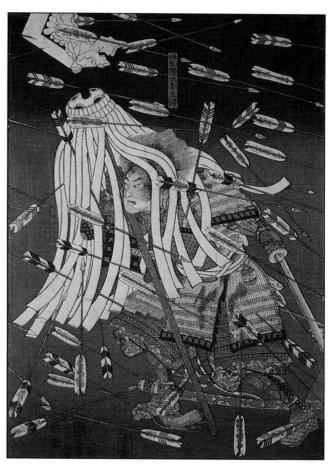

This print from 1861, Last Stand of the Kusunoki Clan, *shows a **samurai** warrior in battle dress.*

THE HEIAN PERIOD lasted from about 790 to 1185 and it is called Heian after the city where the emperor lived. This was a time when power was centered around the court. Landowners were very wealthy, but the rest of society was poor. During this time, Japanese artists and writers began to throw off the influences of China and find their own identity.

THE KAMAKURA PERIOD lasted from about 1185 to 1333. The court at Heian lost its power to the powerful Minamoto **clan**. The leader of the clan, Yoritomo, established himself as the ruler, or supreme **shogun**, of Japan in 1192. A military government called a *bakufu* was set up. Although the emperor kept his court in Kyoto, he had no real **political** power. Yoritomo chose Kamakura as his base because his supporters were mainly warriors of the eastern regions.

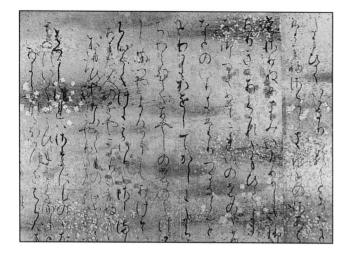

Studying old texts, such as The Tale of Genji, *written in 1010, can help us understand life at that time.*

THE MUROMACHI AND MOMOYAMA periods lasted from 1392 to 1600. The Kamakura era had ended in confusion, with two emperors and two separate courts. For the next 30 years, the two courts were at war. Eventually, the third shogun of the Muromachi *bakufu*, Yoshimitsu, brought the two courts together and political power was centered in Kyoto. However, the *bakufu* was weak, and from 1467 there was a long period of war and unrest. Eventually, Japan was reunified under Toyotomi Hideyoshi. One of the most important cultural features of this time was the rise of **Zen Buddhism** (see page 58).

THE EDO PERIOD began in 1600 and lasted until the beginning of the modern age in 1868. It was named after the city now called Tokyo, where the supreme shogun Tokugawa Ieyasu established himself in 1603. It was a time during which Japan isolated itself from the rest of the world, banning foreigners from entering and stopping the Japanese from traveling abroad.

This Zen "gravel" garden is like a Japanese landscape in miniature.

Japan's isolation came about because the ruling classes feared invasion by other countries and the spread of the Christian religion, which would unsettle Japan's **class structure** (see page 10). It was a period known as "the great peace." Popular arts and crafts flourished, particularly the theater, and people were taught to read and write.

THE MAKE IT WORK! way of looking at history is to ask questions of the past and discover some of the answers by making replicas of the things people made. However, you do not have to make everything in the book to understand the Japanese way of life.

*A samurai wife wears a fashionable **kimono** of the Edo period.*

Timeline

For many centuries Japan was made up of groups of small, independent clans whose chieftains were always at war with each other. In 660 B.C., according to legend, a chieftain called Jimmu defeated the other clans and set up his capital on Honshu island. Jimmu was believed to be a descendant of the sun goddess and became the first emperor of Japan.

IT TOOK MANY CENTURIES before Japan became anything like a unified country. In A.D. 710, the city of Nara became Japan's capital (the capital was sited wherever the ruler had his palace and was usually abandoned after his death). But it was decided that Nara had been built in an unlucky place, so the capital was moved to Heian-kyo in 794. Heian, later known as Kyoto, became the home of the Japanese emperors for over a thousand years. Today, Kyoto is still a strong center for the arts.

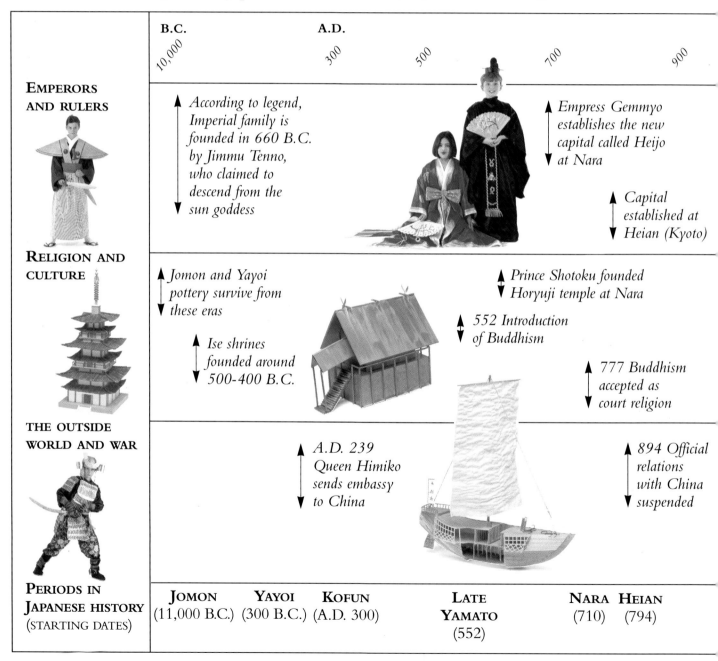

	B.C.	A.D.			
	10,000	300	500	700	900
EMPERORS AND RULERS	*According to legend, Imperial family is founded in 660 B.C. by Jimmu Tenno, who claimed to descend from the sun goddess*			*Empress Gemmyo establishes the new capital called Heijo at Nara* *Capital established at Heian (Kyoto)*	
RELIGION AND CULTURE	*Jomon and Yayoi pottery survive from these eras* *Ise shrines founded around 500-400 B.C.*		*Prince Shotoku founded Horyuji temple at Nara* *552 Introduction of Buddhism* *777 Buddhism accepted as court religion*		
THE OUTSIDE WORLD AND WAR		*A.D. 239 Queen Himiko sends embassy to China*		*894 Official relations with China suspended*	
PERIODS IN JAPANESE HISTORY (STARTING DATES)	**JOMON** (11,000 B.C.) **YAYOI** (300 B.C.) **KOFUN** (A.D. 300)		**LATE YAMATO** (552)	**NARA** (710) **HEIAN** (794)	

THERE WERE LONG STRETCHES of Japanese history when real power was not in the hands of the emperor. From 1190, power passed to the military rulers of Japan, known as the shoguns, and this heralded the age of the samurai warrior. Finally, after centuries of war, three warrior leaders emerged who brought peace to Japan. In 1603, Tokugawa Ieyasu was appointed shogun. His capital, Edo, was one of the largest cities in the world at that time, and his family's rule continued for 14 generations, until 1868.

MODERN TIMES in Japan date from July 1853, when four American warships asked for the right of entry to Tokyo Bay so that trading could take place between Japan and America. Until this time, Japan's rulers had turned down trading requests from foreign governments because they feared invasion and the influence of Christianity. But Japan could no longer survive alone and entry was granted to the U.S. ships. The emperor was restored to power and the country's first **general election** was held in 1890.

A.D.

1000   1200   1400   1600   1800

▲ Minamato Yoritomo establishes military government. Samurai rule begins ▼

▲ Oda Nobunaga conquers central Japan. He is killed 14 years later. Toyotomi Hideyoshi succeeds and unifies Japan ▼

▲ Emperor restored to power in 1868. Court moves to Edo (renamed Tokyo) ▼

▲ Tokugawa Ieyasu takes title of shogun. Tokugawa rule established ▼

▲ The Tale of Genji *written by Murasaki Shikibu* ▼

▲ School of Zen Buddhism founded ▼

▲ Noh theater develops ▼

▲ Growth of Edo, Osaka, and castle towns ▼

▲ Zen culture spreads ▼

▲ Tales of Heike *and other stories about war become popular* ▼

▲ Kabuki, Bunraku, and other arts flourish ▼

▲ 1185 Minamoto clan defeats Taira clan ▼

▲ 1543 firearms introduced ▼

▲ 1635 Japanese banned from traveling abroad ▼

▲ 1853 U.S. ships arrive. Japan opens its ports to foreigners ▼

1639 All Europeans, except a few Dutch traders, told to leave Japan ▼

▲ 1467-77 Onin Wars ▼

KAMAKURA (1185)

MUROMACHI AND MOMOYAMA (1392)

EDO (1600)

MEIJI (1868)

A Land of Contrasts

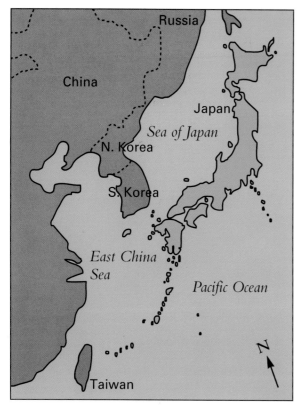

Japan is made up of around 3,900 islands that were once part of the mainland of Asia. They broke off gradually during the last ice age, about 12,000 years ago. There is **archaeological** and **anthropological** evidence that mainland peoples from China and Korea, and Pacific Islanders from the south, continued to migrate to the islands of Japan over thousands of years.

THE FOUR MAIN ISLANDS OF JAPAN – Hokkaido, Honshu, Shikoku, and Kyushu – are heavily forested, with spectacular, sometimes impassable mountains (many of them volcanic), fast-flowing rivers, and fertile plains. Isolated families, or clans, grew up in remote, sheltered valleys. Their **Shinto** religion (see page 56) sprang from their respect for the forces of nature.

◁ *Japan's many islands stretch across 2,400 mi, from the cool north to the semitropical islands of Okinawa in the south. Its neighbors are North and South Korea, China, and Russia.*

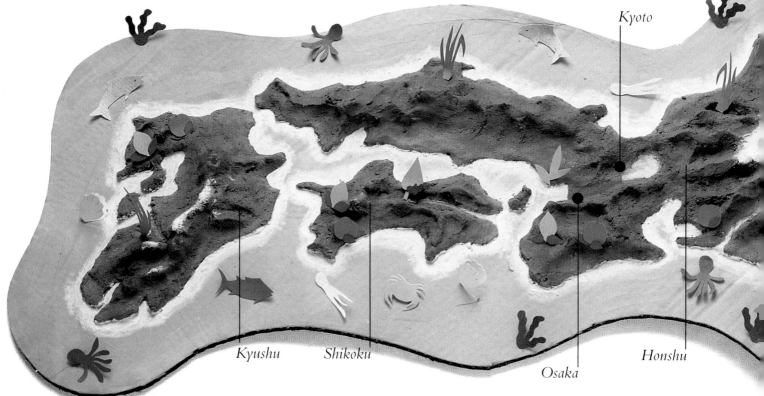

△ *This map shows a few of the crops that are grown on Japan's four main islands and the types of fish that are found in the coastal waters.*

WITH SO MANY MOUNTAINS AND FORESTS, Japan has little grazing land for animals. Rice, fish, and vegetables are its main foods.

rice

seaweed

mulberry bush

tea

oranges

lemons

squid

crab

clam

octopus

salmon

tuna

Hokkaido

THE CLIMATE varies from cool summers and snowy winters in the north to hot, humid summers and cool winters in the south.

EARTHQUAKES AND TYPHOONS are common. There can be 7,000 to 8,000 tremors every year, but most are hardly noticeable. Typhoons strike every year, badly damaging crops and houses.

▽ *Ainu women often tattooed their mouths with soot as a way of warding off evil spirits.*

Edo (Tokyo)

THE AINU PEOPLE of Hokkaido appear to have different origins than the rest of the Japanese population. Not only do they look very different, but their beliefs and language are not the same as the majority. The Ainu were driven out of Honshu where they had settled to Hokkaido. Some experts think the Ainu may have come to Japan from Siberia thousands of years ago, but no one is sure. Very few of the Ainu remain today.

Layers of Wealth and Status

THE TYPE OF CLOTHES worn by Japanese people through history can tell us a lot about society at that time. For example, in the Heian period, nobles had the time and money to worry about the smallest details of their clothing. Their clothes were designed to look good – often at the expense of comfort. For people who worked outdoors, such as farmers, clothes had to be practical, inexpensive, and durable. By the Edo period, wealthy townspeople enjoyed dressing in the latest fashions. The **shogunate** authorities were worried by displays of wealth and made rules to make sure everyone dressed according to their class in **society**.

straw cloak

🐸 **CRAFTSMEN** were ranked below farmers but above merchants, because they made things that were useful, such as samurai swords or cooking pots.

headband

short kimono, or happi coat

straw sandals

farmer's wife

farmer in winter dress

🐸 **FARMERS** were valued in society because they paid taxes to the _daimyo_ in the form of rice and, occasionally, money. Some farmers owned land and were rich, but most were poor workers. Although clothes varied from region to region, farmers usually wore short jackets and trousers made from cotton or hemp. In hot weather, they just wore loincloths – strips of material that went around their hips and between their legs. Women would keep cool by loosening their clothing a little.

craftsman

🐸 **MERCHANTS** were generally despised by the authorities, because they did not actually make anything, but made money by buying and selling the work of others. However, during the Edo period, some grew increasingly wealthy and powerful, while the samurai lost their influence. The authorities tried to stop the merchants from showing off their wealth, by telling them not to wear expensive silks. The merchants got around this rule by lining their cotton robes with silk.

samurai and wife

layers of silk kimonos

over-jacket, or kataginu, with family crest

wide sash, or obi

simple, cotton kimono

kimono

wooden shoes, or geta

divided trousers, or hakama

toe socks, or tabi

silk lining

🐸 **THE SAMURAI** were the highest class in society. They were the only people allowed to carry two swords. They had two types of dress: everyday and ceremonial, shown above.

🐸 **WIVES** of high-ranking samurai put on layers of silk kimonos, with the lighter colors worn underneath. Small, overall patterns were fashionable, as were padded hems that dragged on the floor.

merchant

THE BASIC JAPANESE garment for both men and women was a loose-fitting coat with a tie belt. It is called a kimono, a word that means "the thing worn" and can be used to describe anything from a short smock to the most elaborate gown. Kimonos probably originated in ancient China, and styles and accessories varied through the centuries, according to fashion, the sex, and marital status of the wearer. In general, ordinary people wore simple, practical clothes, increasing the layers according to the season. The ruling classes wore multilayered, fashionable robes to reflect their status in society.

IN THE HEIAN PERIOD, people wore a garment called a *kosode*, a plain T-shaped wrap with short sleeves, with a pair of wide, baggy trousers called *hakama* underneath. Over the years, dress became much simpler and eventually the *kosode* became the outer garment. Once outside, it became highly decorated instead of plain.

△ *Ivory or wooden toggles, called netsuke, were used to anchor small items kept in the waist sash of a kimono. This ivory netsuke is a carving of Hotei, the god of luck.*

MAKE A KIMONO

You will need: dark blue fabric, white fabric, needle and thread, glue, black paint, pins, chalk

1 To make the back panel, lie down on the dark blue fabric and ask a friend to draw a rectangle shape around you with the chalk. The rectangle should flare out slightly at the bottom, as shown above. Cut out the shape carefully.

2 Cut out two front panels as above. They should be the same length as the back panel and half its width. They should curve slightly at the top.

3 Lay the back of the kimono flat on the floor, right side up. Place the front panels on top, right side down, lining up the top and side edges. Sew front and back panels together along the top and down the sides. Leave a gap for the sleeves.

4 Cut out two large sleeve shapes as shown above left. Fold the sleeves in half so that the curved edges meet at the bottom. Sew up the bottom edge and along the curved edge. Leave a gap for your hand to go through.

5 Cut a strip of white material for the neckband, 5 in. wide and long enough to fit along the entire front edge of the kimono, as above.

△ *To make a girl's waist sash, or obi, paint a plain piece of material and wrap it around your kimono twice.*

KIMONOS were carefully picked to match the season or even a particular festival. A plain, elegant style, for example, might be worn for a ceremonial occasion. Artists of the Edo period made woodblock prints showing the latest kimono designs. Ordinary people bought prints to pick up hints on what was fashionable. Kimonos could be worth a lot of money and were an important part of a woman's dowry when she married.

NOBLEWOMEN wore many layers of beautiful silks. On top of red *hakama*, they put on different-colored robes with long sleeves. When they went out in their carriages, they left one sleeve dangling outside, so that everyone who saw them would admire their good taste. For court duties and weddings, from 15 to 40 robes were worn (the larger people were, the wealthier they were thought to be). In the 12th century, the number of robes worn was reduced from 12 to five.

◁ *Nobles often had their family crest embroidered on their clothes.*

family crest, or mon

obi

kimono

6 Line up the edge of the neckband with the edge of the front panels as shown above left. Pin in place, then sew to the panels, keeping your line of stitching about ³/₄ in. from the edge.

7 Turn the sleeves right side out. Slip under the front panel as shown above left, and sew in place, leaving a gap underneath the arm.

8 Turn the kimono right side out. Now fold over the neckband and sew to the front panels, turning the raw edge under as you go. Hem.

9 To make the family crests, called *mon*, cut squares of material and paint on symbols. When the paint is dry, sew or glue the squares onto the kimono.

MAKEUP was also a way of showing how important people were. Both men and women whitened their faces because it distinguished them from tanned and weatherbeaten workers and because a pale face was considered very beautiful. They patted their faces with small cotton bags filled with rice powder, moistened with perfumed water. They also used white lead, and there were many cases of people being poisoned because lead is highly toxic.

THE TYPE OF HAT, or *kammuri*, a man wore was one way to tell what rank he held. The *kammuri* was made of a silk fabric that was **lacquered** and made to look stiff. High-ranking people wore dark or pale violet *kammuri*, while ordinary nobles wore black (see page 23).

WOMEN'S HAIR was considered beautiful if it was long, thick, and shining – like the wing of a raven. Sometimes a woman wore a wig if her real hair did not match this ideal. In the Heian and Kamakura periods, women kept their hair loose, but in other eras it was fashionable to pin it up.

△ *Samurai warriors shaved the tops of their heads, then gathered the hair at the sides and back into a ponytail, which they doubled over and tied tightly.*

MEN'S HAIRSTYLES were another mark of rank. Ordinary workers wore their hair short, while noblemen wore their hair in a topknot. Up until the Edo period, nobles grew mustaches and beards, but samurai kept their faces free of hair. Monks plucked their faces and shaved their heads.

MAKE A PAIR OF JAPANESE SHOES (GETA)

You will need: two pieces of wood, $1/2$" thick; four blocks of wood, $1/2$" thick; string; masking tape; cotton duck; shiny material; paint; strong nails; hammer; glue; hand drill

1 Ask an adult to help cut the wooden base of the shoes, slightly longer and wider than your foot. Cut the corners so they are rounded. For the struts, cut four blocks of wood 2″ deep and as wide as the base.

2 Drill three holes in each base, as shown. Nail two struts to each base, one $1\frac{1}{2}$" from the top, the other $1\frac{1}{2}$" from the bottom. Paint the shoes brown.

3 Cut two rectangles of shiny material as long as the shoe and 4″ wide. Then cut two smaller rectangles of duck. Put the duck on the shiny material and place a length of string in the middle, as shown.

4 Now roll the material and the string up to make two padded tubes, or thongs. Glue the edges down. Glue thin strips of material around the string at the ends of each thong.

5 Pass a string loop through the hole in the front of the shoe. Thread the thong through and knot the loop. Pass the ends of the thong through the remaining holes, knot underneath, and secure with masking tape.

SAMURAI WARRIORS kept their hair neat and tightly tied. It could be very embarrassing if a samurai's hair came undone in battle. And it was considered a terrible disgrace if an opponent lopped off his ponytail.

If a samurai was feeling ill, he would not bother to shave his head. His hair might grow into a messy tangle, but he would be careful never to be seen in public looking like that.

▷ *Apart from haircombs and netsuke, Japanese women did not wear jewelry. Haircombs and pins were made of ivory, horn, wood, or metal and often painted.*

WOMEN reddened their lips with a spot of crushed flower-petal paste on the lower lip to make their mouths look smaller. They also plucked their eyebrows and painted black marks high on their foreheads with a paste of soot and glue. Natural eyebrows were thought to be vulgar, like "fat caterpillars" crawling on the face.

△ *Some hairstyles were very elaborate. To keep them in place, both sexes slept with their heads on padded, wooden headrests instead of pillows.*

The upper classes customarily blackened their teeth, a practice that spread to the other classes over the centuries. As the Japanese had very little calcium in their diet (no milk or cheese), adult teeth were often naturally blackened with decay. Black teeth, therefore, became a sign of maturity, and white teeth were thought to look as "naked as a skinned animal." Married women were the only people who did not blacken their teeth.

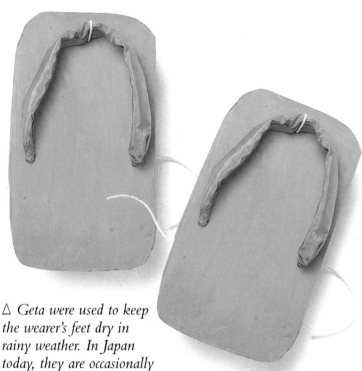

△ *Geta were used to keep the wearer's feet dry in rainy weather. In Japan today, they are occasionally worn with traditional costume.*

FOOTWEAR for ordinary people consisted of thong sandals made of straw. When it rained, they wore *geta,* simple wooden clogs, that kept their feet clear of the mud. Hunters and warriors wore shoes made of leather, and wealthy people wore lacquered wooden *geta* with high platforms and comfortably padded insides. Women who worked in the entertainment world, called **geisha**, wore *geta* so high they could not walk without the help of their servants. Sometimes two-toed, padded cotton socks, called *tabi,* were worn. The thong of the *geta* was slipped between the big toe and second toe.

Living with Nature

Whereas buildings in many parts of the world were built to provide a barrier between people and the outside world, Japanese homes were designed to blend with nature. Natural materials such as wood, bamboo, and paper were used as much for their beauty as their usefulness. Buildings were also made to be adaptable, to cope with the changing seasons.

A TYPICAL FARMHOUSE was a wooden building, one story high. The slope of the thatched roof was steep so that rain or snow would slide off it, and the eaves projected over a verandah so people could stay both cool and dry.

THE BEAMS that made up the wooden frame had interlocking joints. After a typhoon or earthquake, the owner could simply hammer any loose joints back into place.

wooden roof beam

raised living area with sunken hearth, or irori

IN SILKMAKING DISTRICTS, farmhouses were built with a floor under the roof where silkworms were reared on beds of mulberry leaves. Although farmers made the silk, they were not allowed to use it. It was a fabric reserved for the nobility.

shoes

thatched straw roof

wooden ladder for roof repairs

△ _The kitchen was usually situated at ground level. It was full of utensils for cleaning, chopping, and cooking food._

BEFORE MOVING INTO their new house, a family fixed charms to the roof to frighten away demons. Then, a sign with the owner's name on it was hung above the door to show that the family had moved in.

ALL THE VILLAGERS helped each other to build and repair their houses, under the guidance of the village carpenter. The main pillars were set in place (one **ken** apart, about the length of a man lying down) followed by the roof beams. The floorboards were laid on a raised framework, then the sunken hearth, or _irori_, was built. Once the roof was thatched and the outer walls filled in, the house was finished. The villagers held a celebratory feast, with the carpenter as guest of honor.

INTERIORS were very simple. People were more concerned with cleanliness than comfort. They removed their outdoor shoes before stepping onto the raised wooden platform that was the living, eating, and sleeping area. A bucket or tub was conveniently placed at the entrance to wash muddy feet. For preparing food, they kept clean water in a wooden trough at the back of the house.

bucket filled with fresh water

frame for carrying loads

JAPANESE HOMES were designed to adapt to the seasons. In winter, blinds were kept shut and screens, paper walls, and wooden shutters helped to keep the cold out. In summer, these things were swept aside to allow in cooling breezes.

TOWN HOUSES for the merchant class were built close together in rows along the streets, with small gardens at the rear. The houses had similar features to the farmhouses, such as small rooms separated by sliding doors.

MOST ROOMS were used for most purposes. Screens and sliding paper walls could easily be moved and put somewhere else. If the family decided to have a party, for example, they could remove a paper wall to make the room larger.

SCREENS were used to block drafts and for privacy. Most people used screens made of wicker, but in a wealthy home there might be several decorated screens of lacquered bamboo, sometimes framed with gold and encrusted with gems.

MAKE A PAPER SCREEN

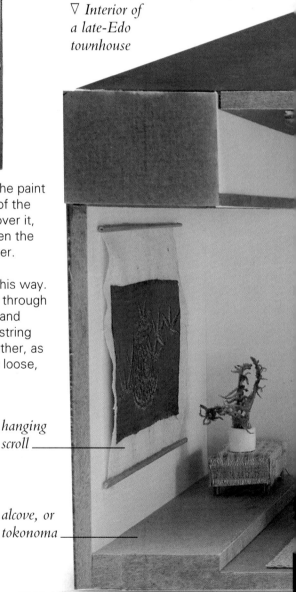

▽ *Interior of a late-Edo townhouse*

You will need: 24 cardboard strips, 23½″ x ½″; 12 cardboard strips, 15¾″ x ½″; masking tape; black paint; string; glue; scissors; white tissue paper, 24″ x 16″.

1 Tape each long strip to another strip of the same length to make 12 extra-thick strips. The screen is made of three panels. To make one panel, tape four short strips horizontally to four long vertical strips, as shown above.

2 Paint the panel black. When the paint is dry, spread glue on one side of the panel and lay the tissue paper over it, keeping it flat and smooth. When the glue is dry, trim the excess paper.

3 Make another two panels in this way. To join the panels, make a hole through the frame and paper at the top and bottom of the screens. Thread string through and tie the panels together, as shown below. Keep the strings loose, so the panels can be folded.

hanging scroll _____

alcove, or tokonoma _____

tatami mat

THE BEST ROOM IN THE HOUSE had an alcove with a raised floor, called a *tokonoma*. This was used to display a piece of pottery or a flower arrangement. On the walls hung a picture or some calligraphy. Originally, a *tokonoma* was reserved for the samurai class, but by the Edo period, it was used by most people.

TATAMI are straw and rush mats made to standard sizes of one *ken* long and half a *ken* wide. Two *tatami* side by side form a square. This was then used to calculate the size of a room.

COOKING EQUIPMENT included oil jars, cauldrons, trays, buckets, bowls, baskets, and boxes, as well as cleavers, a variety of sharp knives, mortars, and pestles. These were all stowed away neatly in wooden chests.

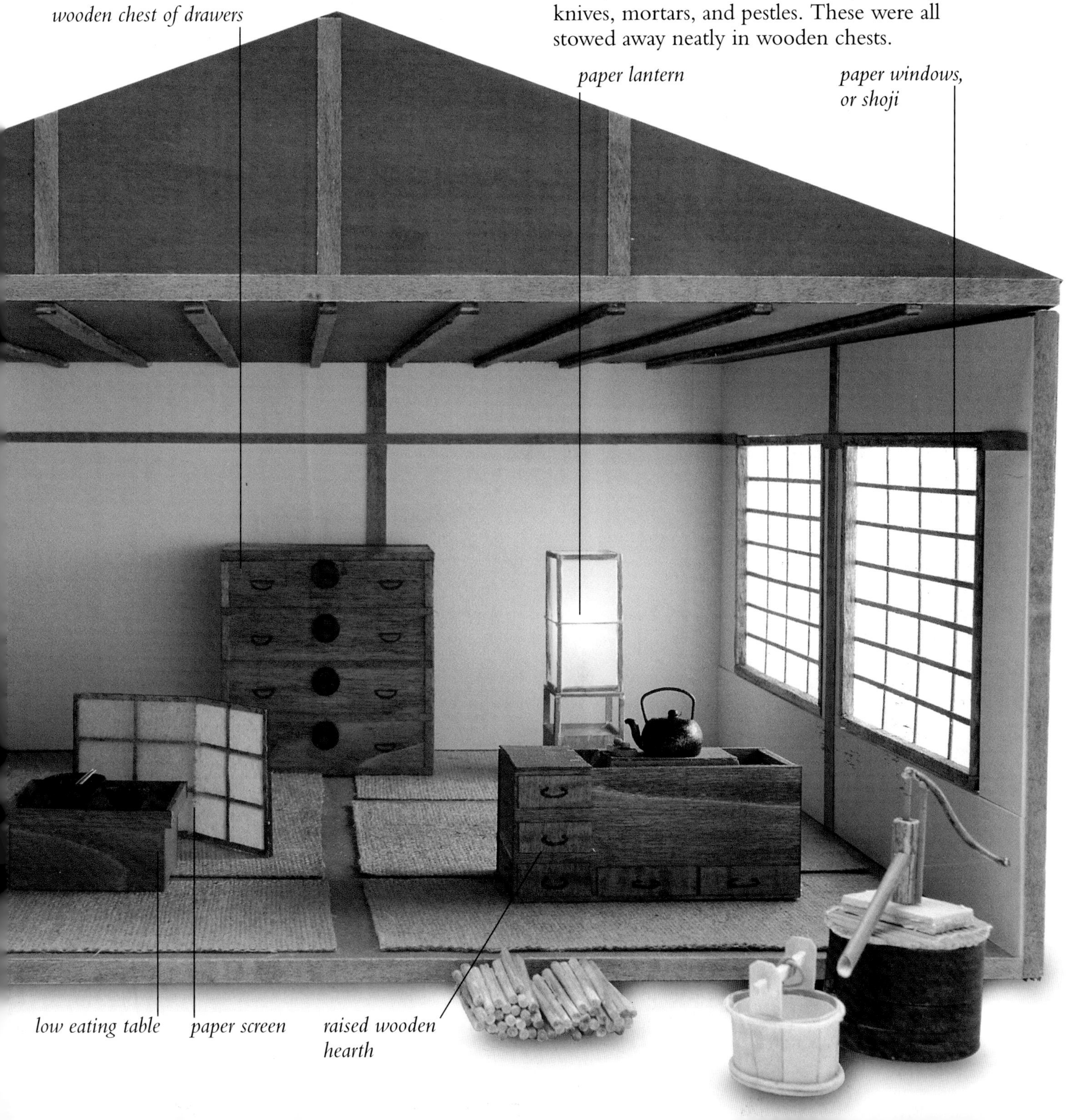

wooden chest of drawers

paper lantern

paper windows, or shoji

low eating table　*paper screen*　*raised wooden hearth*

∆ *Within the castle walls, the daimyo created peaceful gardens where he could contemplate the beauty of nature.*

▽ **THE WALLS** that surrounded the castle and formed the foundations of the keep were built of stones carefully piled on top of each other. The base of the walls curved outward for stability, then rose smoothly and vertically, which made them very difficult to climb. Defense ditches and moats meant that the only way into the castle was over a series of portable bridges, which could be removed in case of attack.

▽ *Castles were usually built on raised mounds, to command and defend the surrounding rice paddies from which the shogun obtained his income.*

▽ **IN THE 16TH CENTURY**, guns and cannons were introduced to Japan. The flimsy, wooden military fortresses, built by the shogun and samurai to keep order in the land, became vulnerable. The shogun had to build permanent castle compounds, with strong stone walls to withstand gunshot and cannonballs.

small keep

windows for throwing stones or boiling water onto the enemy

gaps for firing guns and arrows

gateway to inner courtyard

▽ **TOWNS GREW UP** around the castle walls, and the merchants who supplied the castle and the samurai moved there with their families. These settlements became known as "below the castle towns," and they formed the basis for most major towns in Japan.

NEAR THE SHOGUN'S QUARTERS there were further defense systems. Guards hid in secret chambers, ready to leap out and attack intruders. The floor of the corridor leading to the shogun's rooms was specially made with planks that squeaked. It was known as a "nightingale" corridor because it "sang" if someone tried to creep silently along it.

AT THE HEART of every castle compound was the keep, or *tenshu*. The main keep was usually made up of seven interlinking stories. The doors and screens of the rooms within were decorated by the best artists in the land.

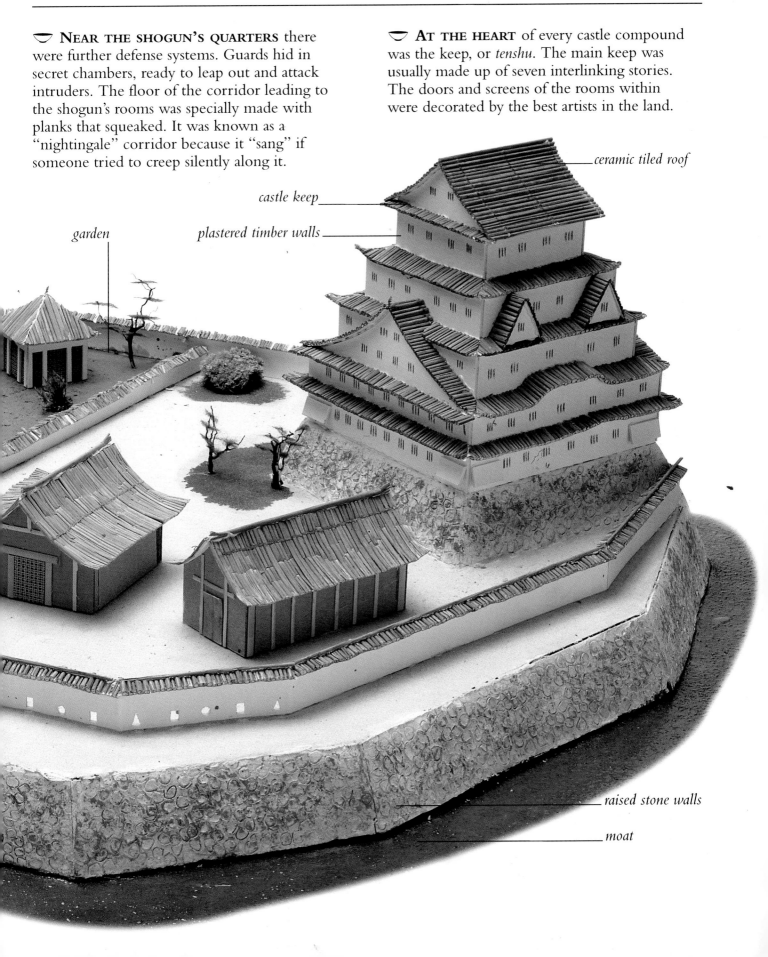

ceramic tiled roof

castle keep

garden

plastered timber walls

raised stone walls

moat

Life at Court

In 794, Emperor Kammu moved his court to a place he called *Heian-kyo*, meaning "capital of peace and tranquility" (now Kyoto). For four centuries court life flourished there. In the early part of this period, courtiers copied the ways of their sophisticated neighbors, the Chinese, but by the year 1000 a distinctly Japanese culture began to appear.

STYLE AND MANNERS were very important in the Heian court. Noblewomen, for instance, wore at least 12 different colored silk robes and spent many hours choosing the colors and deciding in which order to wear them. Getting dressed was a form of art. Paintings from this time often show women elegantly collapsed in a billow of clothing, most likely staggering under the weight of their garments.

MAKE A FAN

2 Lay the strips on top of one another, and pull the thread through the holes at the bottom. Secure the bundle of strips by tying on one button at the front and another at the back.

4 Paint the open fan with a design of a cherry tree in full blossom. When fan is dry, decorate with lengths of braided threads tied to the sides of the fan.

You will need: cream-colored posterboard; paints; paintbrush; two buttons; needle; scissors; drawing compass; colored threads

1 Cut posterboard into 16 tapering strips, 9" long x 1¼" wide at the top. Round off top of each strip, as shown. Use the compass to make a hole in each strip's center at top and bottom, as shown above.

3 Spread the fan out and sew a length of thick thread through the holes in the top of the fan. Knot the thread at either end.

△ *It was the custom for noblewomen to hide their faces from men, so they used beautifully decorated fans as a screen.*

THE MAIN DISTRACTIONS at court were love affairs and religious occasions. People dressed in colorful costumes and sang and danced at the many religious ceremonies. Trips to the countryside became ritualized. Courtiers would travel to see flowers in bloom or to enjoy the smells of different incense woods.

ARISTOCRATIC FAMILIES lived in mansions consisting of a main hall connected to various pavilions by galleries. Their houses were set in landscaped gardens with lakes and little islands and were surrounded by a wall. The pavilions were, like the homes of most people, simply furnished and icy cold in winter. Families ate two main meals, at about 10 A.M. and 4 P.M. Dishes included rice, seaweed, fruit, and vegetables.

LITERARY AND CALLIGRAPHY SKILLS were held in high regard by both sexes. Most nobles wrote poetry, which was especially important for conducting love affairs. Women of the period were known for their elegant novels, diaries, love letters, and poetry. In fact, Japan's earliest and most famous novel, a 1,000-page epic called *The Tale of Genji*, was written by a Heian lady of the court named Murasaki Shikibu. It tells of the life and many loves of a prince.

MARRIAGES between noblemen and women were arranged for the benefit of their families. It was common practice for a wife and her children to remain at home with her family and be visited there by her husband.

▷ *This nobleman and woman show their high rank by wearing costly silks. The man also wears a kammuri, a hat reserved for court members.*

Daily Life in Town

The city of Edo was for a long time the largest and one of the most sophisticated cities in the world. It was a major center for trade and all the main highways converged there. The *daimyo* all had large houses in Edo, and there were temples, shrines, several theaters, a pleasure district, and shops of every kind.

CHILDREN were prepared for their future lives at home. Girls learned how to sew, cook, and wash, while boys learned their father's trade or were sent off to learn the trade of one of his friends. In the spring and summer, children played games outside or went hunting for crickets and fireflies. During the winter months, families spent their evenings together, reading, talking, or playing board games such as **Go**, a game that is still popular in Japan today.

△ *A bathhouse was the perfect place for townspeople to relax. The one above is fed by hot spring water.*

BOYS AND GIRLS were taught to read, write, and do arithmetic in schools that were often attached to temples. Sons of military families were often sent away to be taught by monks or to the homes of even richer families, where they were educated in return for their services as **pages**. Merchants also made sure their daughters were educated, so they could help them run their businesses.

▷ *At New Year, children played with spinning tops made of bamboo and paper.*

MEN were the providers, although women were usually in charge of the family finances. Men were sometimes accused by their wives of wasting the family's money in the city's theaters, restaurants, and bars. However, as heads of the household, men felt they had the freedom to behave as they pleased, whatever their wives said.

WOMEN were expected to do all the housework and cooking, with the help of servants if the family could afford them. Wives served their husbands at mealtimes, but did not eat with them. Among the merchant class, some women owned property and ran businesses and shops. Women were usually very busy with household duties, but occasionally they went on pilgrimages or visited the theater. Many women looked forward to the day when they would have a daughter-in-law to take over the housework.

MOST TOWN HOUSES did not have baths, so public baths were very popular. These were places where men and women could relax and gossip, as well as get clean. As soap was expensive, people used rice bran to wash with instead.

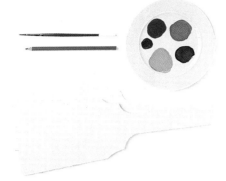

1 Ask an adult to help you cut out four pieces of balsa wood in the shape shown left. They should be 15″ long x 5″ wide at the top.

2 Glue two shapes together to make one bat. Repeat for the other bat. Copy or trace your chosen design onto the bats, as shown above.

3 Paint the handle and the middle section to look like wood. Then color in your design and the stripes. Finally, paint the shuttlecock gold, red, and orange.

You will need: four pieces of balsa wood, pencil, paintbrush and paints, a shuttlecock, craft knife

△ *Originally, battledore was played with a soybean instead of a shuttlecock. Beans were believed to ward off evil and disease.*

CHILDREN LOOKED FORWARD TO several events throughout the year. Perhaps the most enjoyable was New Year, when many games were played. Battledore, or shuttlecock, was a popular New Year's present for girls. Like badminton, the game is played with two people, who try to keep the shuttlecock in the air for as long as possible.

The Warrior Class

During the end of the Heian period, many wars raged throughout Japan. This led to the rise of a group of warrior noblemen called *bushi* (fighting men), or samurai. The samurai had an important influence on Japanese society until the 19th century.

✗ **A WARRIOR GOVERNMENT** seized power from the emperor in the 12th century. Although the emperor and his court continued to live in the capital Kyoto, real power was held by the military ruler, known as the shogun, in the city of Kamakura. The shogun was served by a loyal band of samurai.

▷ *This 17th century samurai dolphin helmet, made from leather, lacquer, and gilt, was meant to make the samurai look impressive, so that he could intimidate the enemy.*

✗ MAKE A SAMURAI SWORD

You will need: cardboard, paper, glue, gold paint, black and white cotton strips, craft knife

1 With an adult's help, cut a curved knife shape 2" x 27" and cut a round hilt, with a slit, from cardboard.

2 Slide the hilt over the sword so that it sits above the blade.

3 Spread glue on both sides of the sword and wrap strips of white cotton around the sword and the hilt as shown above.

4 Paint the sword gold. For the grip, cut two pieces of cardboard. Glue as shown. Wrap with black cotton. Decorate your sword.

🐸 **THE SAMURAI** were fearless fighters who trained for years to learn the skills of swordmanship and archery. The training was very demanding: as well as learning how to fight, the samurai had to go for long periods without food to test their endurance. They were also taught to think and behave in a special way called the *bushido*, or "way of the warrior." By learning the *bushido*, a samurai warrior had an almost religious devotion to carrying out his duties. He was also prepared to die for the shogun, if necessary.

THE SWORD was the samurai's most valuable possession and was handed down from father to son. Those who made swords were highly respected and even dressed in the white robes of a Shinto priest. Sword blades were made of a combination of hard and soft metal and were so sharp that they could behead an enemy with a single blow. Sword guards, or *tsubas*, were beautifully decorated, to reflect the skill needed to make the blade.

▷ *The samurai wore light and loose-fitting clothes, so they could move quickly in battle. Armor was worn over the top for protection.*

helmet with horns to frighten the enemy

neck shields

SAMURAI ARMOR was made of hundreds of scales of lacquered iron. These scales were tied together in rows with silk cord. The way they were linked together made the armor very strong, giving the samurai the protection they needed.

△ *This 19th century Japanese sword guard shows three holy men, **Confucius**, **Buddha**, and Lao-Tse, tasting rice wine beneath a pine tree.*

breastplate

WHEN FACING THE ENEMY, the samurai performed a number of rituals. Each warrior announced his name, family background, and a list of brave deeds he had done. Then the battle would begin. The victor praised his enemy before cutting off his head. In case his life should end in the same way, a samurai always burned incense in his helmet, so that if his head was cut off in battle, it would still smell sweet!

sword hangs from the waist

iron-scale armor

🐸 **FOR HUNDREDS OF YEARS** the samurai were valued for their skill at warfare. During the Edo period, peace spread throughout Japan, and the samurai became more involved with administrative duties and matters of ceremony than with fighting.

boots made of leather or bearskin with studded soles

Seasons and Celebrations

Life for the Japanese followed the rhythms of nature strictly. Different foods were eaten according to the season, and homes were rearranged to cope with the changing weather. Even the Japanese calendar of celebrations and festivals was based on ancient ceremonies to mark the yearly planting, growing, and harvesting cycles.

MAKE A CARP STREAMER

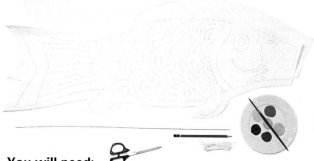

You will need: thin paper, paintbrush, paint, masking tape, glue, scissors, string, length of thin, flexible cane

1 Lay two sheets of thin paper on top of each other. Draw a fish shape, including fins and tail, as above.

2 Cut out the shape and paint the fish on one side of each piece of paper. Gluing the edges only, stick the two plain sides of the fish together. Leave the mouth and tail unglued.

3 Tape the cane into a circle and place it inside the fish's mouth. Fold the fish's lips over it and tape in place. Tie string to the hoop to hang or fly your carp.

△ *During the Doll Festival, girls give parties for their friends and enjoy special candies and drinks.*

SPRING begins in the cold of early February when the plum trees bloom and ends with Boys' Day on May 5.

▷ *Families with sons hung carp streamers from poles outside their homes on Boys' Day.*

BOYS' DAY was originally a festival to prepare farm laborers for the hard work of transplanting rice seedlings. In Heian times it was known as the sweet flag festival (named after a type of plant), and people hung out branches of sweet flag to keep evil away from their homes. As the stem of sweet flag looks like a sword, the ceremony gradually became a celebration of martial arts. By the Edo period, the festival was associated with symbols of manliness and courage. The paper carp that hang from flagpoles today on Boys' Day are symbols of courage and ambition, in recognition of an age-old tale of a carp that once swam all the way to heaven to become a dragon. Displays of dolls are also common today, with models of folk heroes, warriors, and emperors.

THE DOLL FESTIVAL was celebrated on March 3 in households where there were daughters. In Edo times, a whole room was used to display the dolls, principally the emperor and empress in Heian costume. As well as celebrating daughters, the festival was supposed to ward off evil spirits.

REFRESHING FOODS, such as cold soups, noodles, and **tofu**, were served on white or glass plates in summer. Juicy fruits were also popular.

ROOMS WERE KEPT COOL by hanging bamboo or cloth blinds that allowed cooling breezes in but kept out the glare of the summer sun.

▽ *Candlelit lanterns were used in summer to cast moving shadows on the walls. This gave the effect of being in a cool, shady forest.*

SUMMER starts in early May, when misty rains fall for about four weeks. Crops grow thick and fast, and it is very humid. In July, the heat is almost unbearable. Gifts of cooling foods, such as watermelon, are sent with greetings to mark the end of summer on August 7. *Obon* is the main holiday of the season, based on an ancient custom of welcoming the souls of ancestors.

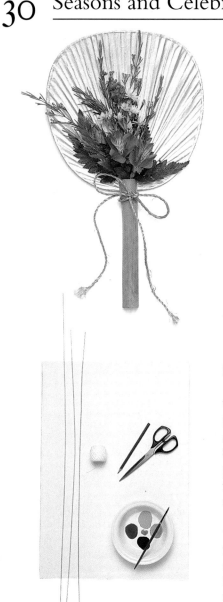

THE MOON FESTIVAL was celebrated in August. In the Heian period, parties of people went out at night to view the moon and make up poems praising its beauty. Musical instruments were played gently in the background to make the occasion even more special.

AUTUMN was seen as a welcome release from the heat of summer. The Japanese went on special trips to see the most colorful displays of autumn leaves. The fading beauty of autumn has also inspired much Japanese poetry and painting.

◁ *This fan represents the full moon and is decorated with autumn flowers and leaves.*

MAKE A KITE

You will need:
lengths of flexible cane: $3/4$" x 30" long, $3/8$" x 38" long, string, paint, masking tape, glue, thin paper, scissors, doweling or bamboo

1 To make the kite frame, tape the ends of the shorter lengths of cane together to make a large loop, as shown right. Then cross the ends of the long piece of cane and tape them together, as above.

2 Tape the crossed length of cane on top of the loop. Place the cane frame on the paper and trace around the shape, drawing a square to cover the crossed cane at the bottom. Allow an extra $3/8$" all around to fold over the frame.

3 Draw and paint your design on the paper, as shown above. (You can use the large image on the right as your guide.) Let dry thoroughly.

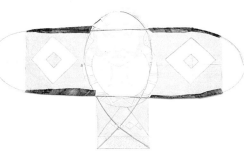

4 Cut out the design and place on the frame. Trim the edges and glue in place. Now tie two pieces of string from the top to the bottom of each wing. Stretch a piece of string across the wings to curve the kite.

5 Cut three pieces of string, 14" long. Tie one to the top of each wing and the third to the center of the body. Tie the loose ends to a long string, wound onto a piece of dowel or bamboo.

Most people had several days holiday over New Year. However, there was a lot of work to do during the weeks before New Year, especially for women. It was important that the whole house was cleaned and enough food prepared to last the whole holiday, so that no cooking was necessary. It was also traditional to pay off all the household debts by the end of the old year, so the next year could be started fresh.

△ *Kites were either decorated with fierce-looking warriors from ancient legends or with animal figures.*

NEW YEAR was, and still is, the biggest festival of the Japanese year. Lots of games are played at this time, and in the Edo period making and flying paper kites was very popular. As well as being fun, kite-flying had a religious significance. The kite was seen as a link between heaven and earth, so that when a kite was sent up into the sky, the Japanese believed they were sending a prayer up to the gods.

Many of the traditions associated with New Year are still followed today. As the temple bells welcomed in the new year at midnight, people ate noodles to ensure a long life. Some people went to watch the sun rise from a nearby mountain, and many people visited temples or shrines during the holiday period.

Different types of food were eaten during New Year. Homemade rice cakes, called *mochi*, were very popular. Each member of the family took turns pounding the cakes into the right shape and texture. They also offered the cakes to the gods of the household and to their ancestors by placing several cakes on the Buddhist and Shinto altars in the house.

Rice, Fish, and Vegetables

Japan is a country of steep mountains, which makes growing crops very difficult. It also means that there is only a small amount of land available for farming. Despite the problems, rice was introduced in the first century and has remained the staple food of the Japanese ever since.

PLANTING, GROWING, AND HARVESTING RICE is hard and time-consuming work. All the people in a village gathered together to help plant and harvest this vital crop.

THE RICE CYCLE BEGAN at the end of spring when a small patch of land was prepared for sowing the rice seed. The seeds were sown at the beginning of May, while the main fields were plowed and flooded. When the seedlings reached around 12 inches high, they were ready to be planted.

AT THE START OF THE RAINY SEASON, all the villagers would help plant the seedlings. It was back-breaking work. The planters were often young women, as it was thought their fertility would bring a bountiful crop. They sang as they worked, planting neat rows of rice in the paddies.

▽ *This model shows the stages of rice growing, from planting in spring to harvesting and drying in autumn.*

carrying seedlings to the planters

treadmill brings water into fields

stripping, or heckling, the harvested rice

AS THE PLANTS GREW, they had to be kept clear of weeds and the water level checked constantly. If water was scarce, the farmers would argue over their share, and some might even divert water away from a neighbor's fields into their own.

harvesting the rice using sickles

HARVESTING took place around October or November. The water was allowed to drain away from the field, and then sickles were used to cut down the rice. The long sheaves of rice were gathered into bundles or circular stacks and left to dry in the sun. Then the grain was stripped, or heckled, by pulling the plant between two sticks or hitting the plant against a large, open barrel. The remaining grain was winnowed, or separated, by being thrown up into the air. The farmer was left with brown, or unpolished, rice still covered in its outer husk. Once the harvest was complete, the tax collector visited each farm to calculate the *daiymo*'s share of the rice.

young rice plants

raised bank or dike separates the paddy fields

rice seedlings planted in flooded paddy field

🐸 **DIFFERENT METHODS** were used to keep the precious rice crop healthy. Some, such as spraying the fields with a mixture of whale oil and vinegar, were quite effective against hungry pests. Other methods included magic rituals or offering prayers to the gods to bring rain.

△ *Over the centuries, farmers developed several ingenious methods of irrigation, such as the waterwheel shown above.*

Japan is surrounded by sea and has many lakes and rivers, so fish has always been an important part of the Japanese diet, providing much-needed protein. As well as sea and river fish, shellfish and even seaweed were collected and eaten. Fish was sometimes cooked, but was also enjoyed sliced and eaten raw.

FISHERMEN worked either part-time or full-time. Those who worked part-time spent most of the year farming and only fished during the season. Full-time fishermen spent every day, weather permitting, going out to sea or along the rivers and mending their nets and boats. Their wives would often help to support the family by growing some rice and vegetables.

LARGE FLEETS OF FISHING VESSELS set sail from the coasts around Edo. They were financed by the merchants and brought back daily catches that were sold as soon as they were unloaded. Ordinary people often fished in local lakes and rivers to supplement their basic diet.

▽ *Women gathered different types of seaweed and shellfish from the seashore to eat or sell at the market.*

mooring pole ———

△ *Cormorant fishermen suspended small fires in buckets from the bow of their boats to attract fish.*

ON SOME RIVERS, cormorants were trained to dive in the water and snap up the fish. A metal or rope ring around the birds' necks stopped them from swallowing, so the fishermen could retrieve the catch from their mouths.

thwart

bow

straw matting used for grip

scoop net

△ *On this boat, the fishing net was attached to the boat and carefully lowered into the water. After a while, the fishermen raised the net and scooped out any fish caught in the net.*

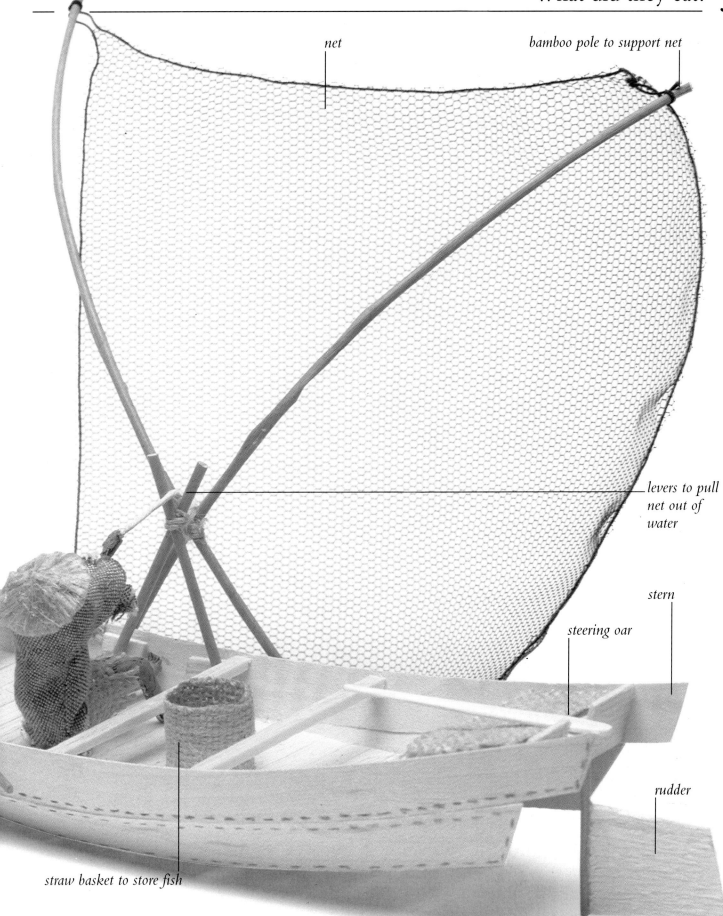

net

bamboo pole to support net

levers to pull
net out of
water

stern

steering oar

rudder

straw basket to store fish

THERE WERE MANY RITUALS attached to eating and drinking in Japan. Much care was taken with the preparation of food and drink. A lot of time and imagination went into making food look as attractive as possible, by choosing different colors and textures of food and arranging the food on beautiful plates and in small bowls.

FISH, rather than meat, was the main source of protein for most people. It could be eaten in many different ways: boiled, grilled, or cut into thin slices and dipped in **soy sauce** and eaten raw. Another popular dish was *sushi*: raw fish rolled in vinegared rice and then wrapped in a sheet of seaweed.

TEA ARRIVED from China in the ninth century. At first it was used as a medicine, but by the 14th century nobles and samurai drank it at social gatherings. It was not until a century later that tea became a popular drink for everyone. Then, it was sipped at the end of a meal to wash down the last few grains of rice.

DRINKING RICE WINE, or *sake*, was enjoyed by men and women, and there were several customs associated with drinking it. Sake was served only during the first part of the meal. It was considered very rude to pour your own, so people took turns pouring sake for one another.

MAKE SUSHI

You will need: vinegared rice; tofu; chopped, cooked mushrooms; crab sticks; cucumber; avocado; smoked salmon; a sheet of seaweed (*nori*) or steamed cabbage leaves; soy sauce; thin cane table mat

1 Place the seaweed on the cane mat. Cover all of the seaweed with rice, apart from one edge. Lay the other ingredients in strips across the rice.

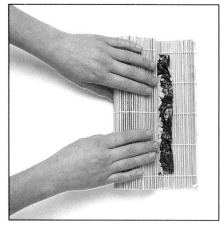

2 Use the mat to roll the seaweed into a tube. The rice should be wrapped around the other ingredients.

3 Unroll the mat. Slice the seaweed roll into pieces 1 1/2″ across. Now dip your sushi into the soy sauce and eat it.

CHOPSTICKS, or *hashi*, have been used in Japan for over a thousand years. They were usually made of wood, but they could also be made of ivory, bone, silver, or gold. Extra long chopsticks were used for cooking and serving food. In Japan, chopsticks are pointed at one end, but in China they are blunt.

1 Hold the first chopstick between your thumb and first finger. Rest it lightly against your middle and third finger.

2 Hold the second chopstick between your thumb and first finger, resting it against your first and middle fingers.

3 Try to keep the first chopstick still and move the second chopstick up and down, so that the pointed ends touch each other.

◁ *The type of hand-rolled sushi shown here was first eaten toward the end of the Edo period. But raw fish, dipped in soy sauce, and called sashimi, dates back even further.*

Getting Around

Traveling in Japan before the Edo period was difficult. Steep mountains and rivers and heavy rains and typhoons made traveling hazardous. A few determined people traveled on official business or made pilgrimages to holy shrines. It was not until the Edo period, when highways provided safer and more convenient links between towns and cities, that travel became easier for more people.

DURING THE HEIAN PERIOD, there were very few good roads, and bands of robbers made them unsafe to travel. However, nobles from the capital still ventured out on trips, either to see the cherry blossom or to visit a local shrine.

△ *Due to the rough conditions of the highways, and many mountains and rivers, most people traveled on foot.*

△ *The palanquin was a type of bamboo box suspended from two poles. It was supported by men who were paid to carry passengers.*

THE MAIN FORMS OF TRANSPORTATION were the palanquin and the slow and uncomfortable ox-drawn carriage. Carriages were a status symbol, and there were many rules about the kind of carriages that low- or high-ranking nobles could travel in. Nobles competed with each other by showing off their beautiful carriages. The imperial family traveled in the most elaborate carriage, which had a green gabled roof and was so high that a ladder was needed to climb into the seat.

▷ *This type of carriage was used mainly by the nobility at the time of the Heian court.*

TRAVEL BECAME EASIER during the Edo period, as more roads were built connecting major centers. Ordinary people traveled for business as well as pleasure. Nevertheless, people could not travel wherever and whenever they wanted. They needed special papers from the authorities, which were checked by officials at certain intervals on the main routes.

THE TOKAIDO, or eastern sea road, was one of the most important highways at this time. It stretched from the city of Edo to Kyoto, providing a vital communication link between the cities. Messengers ran along the highway in relay teams, carrying important letters or money from one city to another. Those running on business for the authorities carried lanterns marked "official business" and were given special treatment at checkpoints and ferries.

DAIMYO and their servants frequently traveled in processions from their estates to the capital, Edo. As the processions passed along the highways, ordinary people had to show their respect by moving to the side of the road and dropping to their knees. Post-stations, where the nobles could hire horses and porters, were placed at regular intervals along the highway .

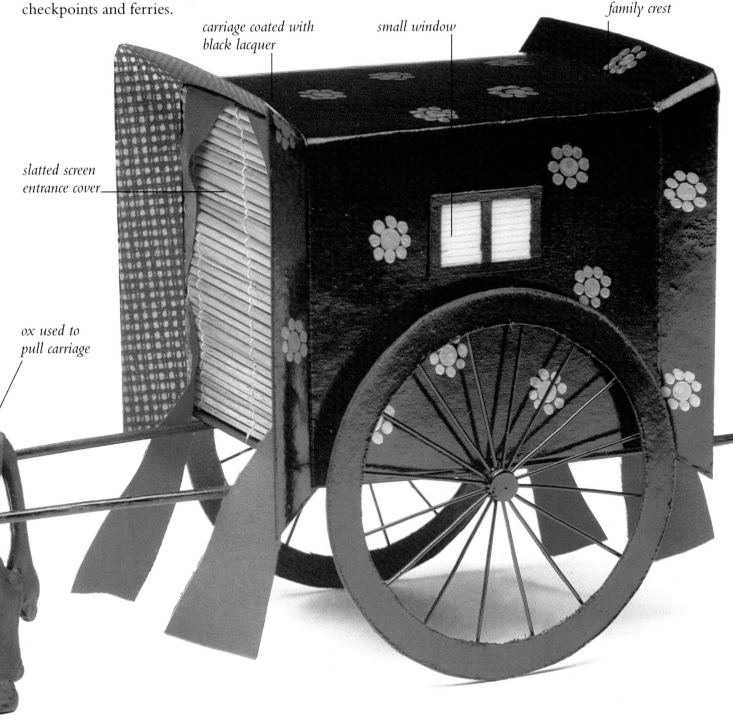

carriage coated with black lacquer

small window

family crest

slatted screen entrance cover

ox used to pull carriage

Transportation and Trade

With the growth of towns and large cities like Edo, and Osaka to the southwest, trade flourished. Improved methods of transportation by road and sea meant that merchants were able to move their goods more easily around the country. Despite the authorities' attempts to stop the growing power of the merchant class, many merchants became very wealthy.

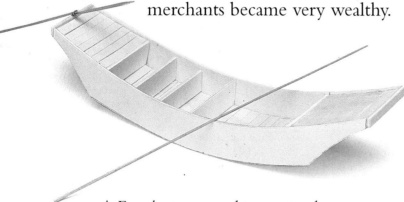

△ Ferry boats were used to carry travelers across rivers. If there were no ferry boats, a porter would wade across the river, carrying travelers and their belongings for a small fee.

🐸 TRADE INCREASED inside Japan, both by road and sea. Waterways in particular were very important in the city of Edo. A system of canals was used not only to move people from place to place, but also to move goods by barges from warehouses to different parts of the city. As the city grew larger, more bridges were built. The most famous bridge was called Nihonbashi.

△ Nihonbashi, "the bridge of Japan," was the meeting place of the five main highways in the city of Edo.

🐸 DURING THE EDO PERIOD, trade with the outside world was very restricted. Japanese ships did not sail to other countries, and in 1635 the Japanese were forbidden to go abroad. A few Chinese and Dutch traders were allowed to live on a small island off Kyushu. As these were the only foreigners allowed inside Japan, the Japanese were naturally very curious about them. The Dutch traders were known as "red hairs" because of their light-colored hair. Some Japanese people even thought that they had hoofs instead of feet.

SMALL JUNKS OR COASTAL SHIPS transported goods around the country, moving cargo from harbor to harbor. One of the most important trade routes was between the cities of Osaka and Edo; large cargoes of rice, sake, and soy sauce were ferried back and forth.

bamboo poles crisscrossed over cargo

large sail made
of hemp

◁ *The oban was a large, gold coin that was used mainly by samurai or wealthy merchants or at special ceremonies.*

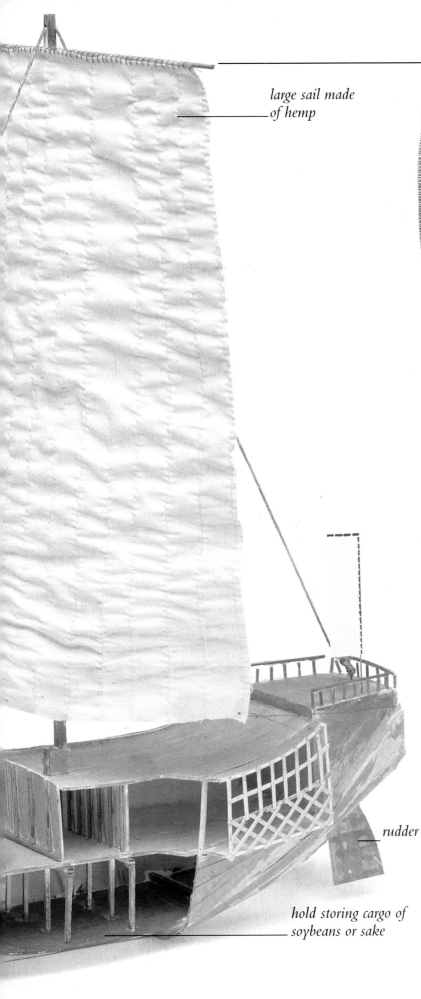

MERCHANTS grew increasingly important as Edo and Osaka became much more commercial. As well as opening shops in the cities, merchants acted as money-lenders to the samurai and made profits on the loans. They also played important roles as money changers, converting rice into money and even lending money to the *daimyo* against delivery of rice crops. A result of all this trade was that the merchants became very powerful economically.

MONEY was hardly ever used by the majority of people. Instead, people relied on trade. They would trade goods for rice, or sometimes swapped valuable objects, such as musical instruments or clothes, for the things or service they needed.

Using money was complicated, as gold, silver, copper, and iron were all used for making coins in different parts of the country. For example, gold was used in the city of Edo, but in Osaka and Kyoto silver coins were common. For everyday purchases in shops most people used small copper coins that they kept tucked into the folds of their kimonos.

rudder

hold storing cargo of
soybeans or sake

◁ *One of the main shipping lines was the Higaki, or "diamond line," so called because of the diamond-shape pattern on the ship. The pattern was made by bamboo poles that were crossed over the cargo to stop it from falling overboard.*

A Rich, Cultural Life

In early Japanese history, music and dance were more often associated with religious ceremonies. Gradually, music and dance became accepted forms of entertainment. In the Heian period, music from Korea, China, and India was also popular in court.

IN THE HEIAN COURT, music and dance were very important to the nobles. They were an essential part of court rituals and everyday life. An educated person was expected to know how to dance or play a musical instrument. It was also believed that if people danced, played, or sang well, they would reveal their true characters.

MAKE A DECORATIVE SHAMISEN

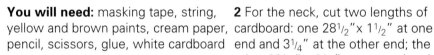

You will need: masking tape, string, yellow and brown paints, cream paper, pencil, scissors, glue, white cardboard

1 For the body, cut two 7³/₄″ rounded cardboard squares. Cut four cardboard rectangles 7³/₄″ x 2¹/₂″. Tape three to one square, making an open box.

2 For the neck, cut two lengths of cardboard: one 28¹/₂″ x 1¹/₂″ at one end and 3¹/₄″ at the other end; the other 23¹/₂″ x 3¹/₄″ at one end and 6¹/₂″ at the other end. Draw five lines along the short length. Score, using scissors and bend to shape. Tape neck pieces together and fix to body.

3 Add last rectangle and square to close up body. For the peg head, cut two shapes from cardboard as shown above. Make three slits in each. For tuning pegs, cut three cardboard strips. Pass through slits and glue in place. For the fret, cut a thick piece of cardboard 1¹/₂″ long. Glue across top of neck.

MUSIC AND DANCE played an important part in village festivals. A whole village would gather to sing folk songs and dance. Often the songs and dances were special to that region of Japan. Some of the men and women would dance in circles, while other members of the village played flutes and drums or sometimes the *shamisen*.

FOLK SONGS have a long history in Japanese music. From the Kamakura period, groups of blind minstrels would wander the country singing tales of famous battles. The *Tales of Heike* was famous and told the story of two powerful families, the Taira and the Minamoto clans, who fought during the 12th century. Minstrels played on a type of lute called a *biwa* while singing these tales to their audience.

◁ *Drums of all sizes are used to accompany traditional music at festivals all over Japan.*

THE SHAMISEN came to Japan from Okinawa in the late 1500s. At first the *shamisen* was played by blind lute players, but it quickly became a favorite instrument in the entertainment districts of cities. It was widely used in **Kabuki** theater and by female entertainers called *geisha* and was also popular with ordinary townspeople.

GEISHA were women trained from an early age to entertain by singing, dancing, playing the *shamisen*, and even talking in a witty and elegant manner. Famous *geisha* were like movie stars, and their skills at music and dance were greatly appreciated. They often had several maids who might also be training to become *geisha*.

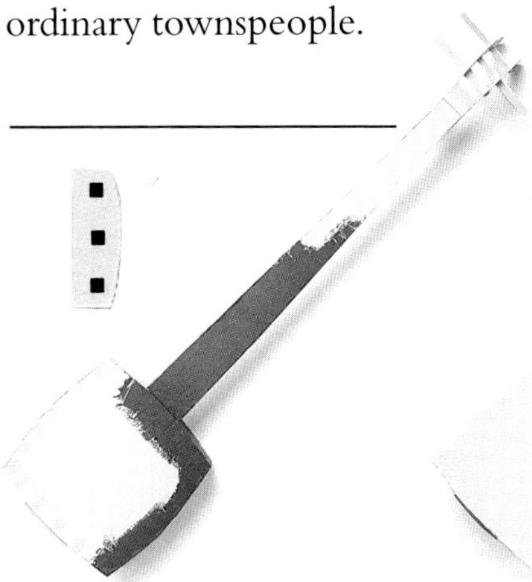

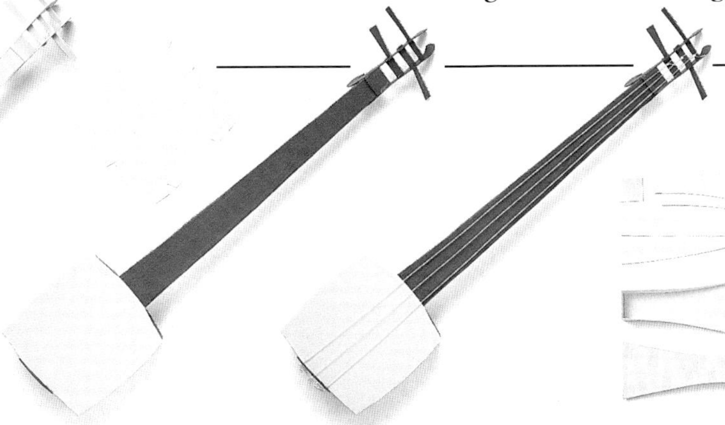

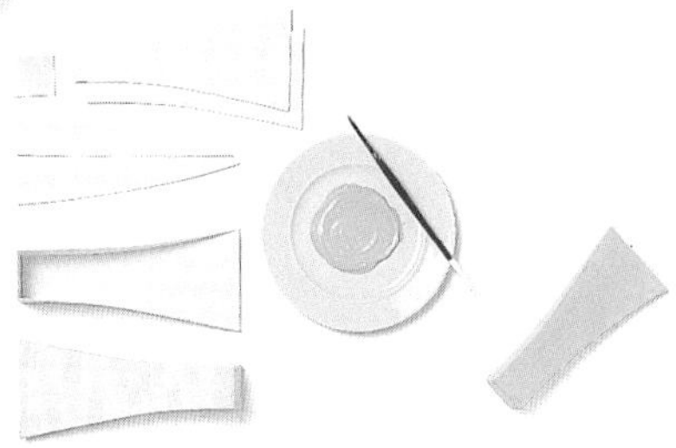

4 Slide the peg head over the end of the neck and glue in position.

5 For the bridge, cut an arched rectangle of cardboard, $3\frac{1}{4}" \times 1\frac{1}{2}"$, as above. Make three holes in the top of the arch. Now glue to end of the body. Paint the *shamisen* brown.

6 Cut a large square of cream paper and glue over the body.

7 Tie three strings to the tuning pegs. Pass the strings over the fret and tie to the bridge at the end of the *shamisen* body.

8 To make the plectrum, cut shapes out of the white cardboard as shown above. Tape the pieces together and paint yellow.

tuning pegs
fret
peg head
neck

body
plectrum
bridge

◁ *The shamisen has three strings, which are strummed. It is used to accompany puppet chanters in a type of theater known as* **Bunraku**.

Noh theater has its origins in rituals that were connected with the rice harvest and with entertainment in Buddhist temples.

In performance, the actor moves in a slow, elegant fashion across an almost bare stage. Four musicians sit at the back of the stage and accompany a group of people who chant a story in a solemn way. This chant tells a story as the performance unfolds. The main character often wears a mask that represents a certain type of person, perhaps a young man or maybe a ghost. The expression on the mask tells the audience if the character is sad, jealous, or angry.

Originally, Noh theater was not intended for ordinary people, but was only for the nobles and samurai. It became so popular among some high-ranking lords that they would invite Noh actors to their homes to perform and would even take part in the performance themselves.

◁ Noh masks are thought to have a religious significance. This is the mask of Okina, the holy sage. The Okina mask is worn in a special dance, where prayers for peace and fertility are offered.

MAKE A NOH MASK

You will need: paint, paintbrush, sandpaper, strips of newspaper, wallpaper paste, string, wool, masking tape, balloon

1 Blow up the balloon. Cover one half with several layers of newspaper strips soaked in the paste. Use the paper and paste to form a nose.

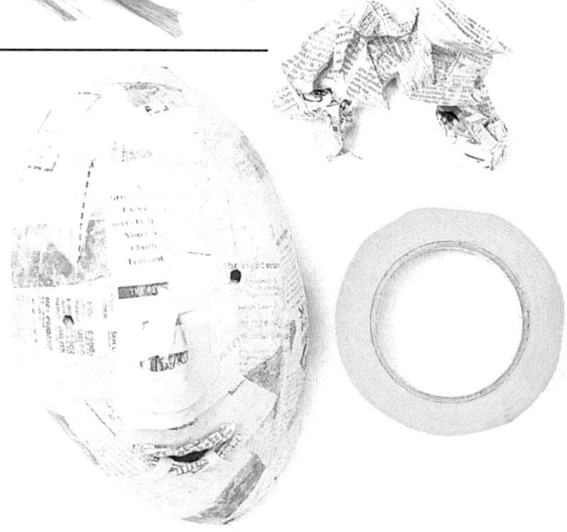

2 When the mask is dry, pop the balloon and smooth any rough edges with sandpaper. Cut out two holes for the eyes, halfway up the mask.

Bunraku was a form of theater popular during the Edo period. The stars of Bunraku were not actors, but half life-sized puppets. While the puppets provided all the movements on stage, someone offstage sang in a chantlike way, telling the story and providing the voices of the puppets.

Two or three puppet masters, dressed in black, controlled the movements of the puppets onstage. The puppets made all kinds of happy and sad expressions, as even their eyeballs and eyebrows could be moved. A musician would play the *shamisen* to accompany the voices of the chanters.

🐸 KABUKI THEATER began in 1586 when, according to legend, a woman called Okuni danced in a dry river bed in Kyoto. Before long, Kabuki performances became very popular and drew huge crowds. The authorities were afraid of trouble breaking out among the audience, so they passed various laws banning young boys and women from taking part in Kabuki. They thought that this would put a stop to the performances. But adult male actors took on the women's roles and soon became so skilled that their beautiful appearance and costumes often set the style for fashion in the cities.

Kabuki performances were very lively and colorful, recounting tales from Japanese history, adventures of superhuman heroes, and love stories. During the play, members of the audience would shout out words of praise or even rude comments to the actors.

▷ *Kabuki actors start their training at a very early age. They have to learn all the roles and every aspect of Kabuki movement, makeup, and costume.*

THE ENTRANCES AND EXITS of a Kabuki actor were very exciting. The actors were famous for striking dramatic poses, flinging their heads and arms around and stamping their feet. Some costumes were designed to look oversized and colorful, to give the actor a larger-than-life presence on stage.

3 Paint the mask with several coats of white paint. When the paint has dried, draw the outline of the eyes and nose in black and the lips in red.

4 To make the Okina mask opposite, add tufts of wool for eyebrows and pieces of string to make a beard.

THE SHOGUNATE AUTHORITIES thought that the plays and actors set a bad example for ordinary people. They passed laws that treated the actors and other entertainers almost like criminals. Samurai were discouraged from attending Kabuki plays, but sometimes they would disguise themselves and sneak into the theater.

THE NOBLES had a great deal of free time during the Heian period. Games and sports were an important way for them to amuse themselves, although some games and sports were more than just entertainment. **Sumo** wrestling contained important rituals that were part of Shinto belief; the referee even wore the costume of a Shinto priest. Other sports were practiced for very practical reasons. **Martial arts** such as **karate**, **kendo**, and **judo** were developed to help a warrior improve the skills he needed in battle. As well as developing physical fitness, all of the martial arts required strong concentration and mental discipline.

KENDO, which means "the way of the sword," was developed so that the samurai could keep up with sword practice. By the 14th century there were several schools teaching kendo. The spontaneous moves and rituals of kendo went hand in hand with the Zen Buddhist idea of *mushin*, or "no mind." Rivals moved so quickly that they did not have time to think, but had to rely on their reflexes.

MAKE A KENDO MASK

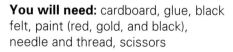

You will need: cardboard, glue, black felt, paint (red, gold, and black), needle and thread, scissors

1 Cut two or three long strips of cardboard, 1″ wide, and glue together.

2 Curve the strip into an oval shape that is large enough to fit over your face.

3 Cut another strip, 1″ wide, and glue it lengthwise along the oval.

4 Glue short strips across the oval, curving them outward, as above.

5 Paint the oval shape red and the other strips black. When dry, paint a gold line on top of each black strip.

SUMO WRESTLING is the most ancient sport in Japan. Originally, wrestlers fought in a small ring in Shinto shrines during festivals. The object was to make the opponent touch the ground with a part of his body, other than his feet, or fall out of the ring. From about 1780, meetings were held over 10 days, and wrestlers were ranked according to their ability. Eventually, sumo stadiums were built, and popular wrestlers were as famous as the great Kabuki actors.

◁ *Shinto rituals play an important part in sumo: a wrestler must wear his hair and belt in a precise way.*

△ *Opponents sit in this crouching position before and after combat.*

◁ *This position is good for both attack and defense.*

IN KENDO TODAY, instead of using a sword, a long bamboo pole called a shinai is used. Those who practice kendo are known as kendo-ka. Action is so swift that it is impossible to prepare moves in advance.

◁*The "cut" is a position of attack.*

6 For the hood, place two pieces of black felt together. Cut out the shape as shown above. Place the mask on the felt and cut around it to make the correct size gap for your face.

7 Sew both pieces of felt together along the back of the hood.

8 Turn the hood inside out. Glue the mask to the inside edge of the hood or sew for extra strength.

△ *It is important to hold the shinai with a firm grip.*

 JUDO, "the way of gentleness," comes from a martial art called *ju-jitsu*, which involves opponents trying to wrestle each other to the ground. It started as a form of unarmed self-defense and was popular in the late Edo period. By 1911 it was widely taught in schools all over Japan.

KARATE did not actually reach mainland Japan until the 1920s. Originating in China, the word *karate* means "empty hand." The fists and feet are used for fighting instead of weapons.

◁ ▷ *While sparring, oponents keep their eyes constantly trained on one another.*

A Living Language

Nobody is very sure where the Japanese language comes from. One theory is that it is related to Korean; another is that it originates from a group of languages that come from central Asia. The way Japanese was spoken varied from region to region. In northern Japan, the Ainu people spoke a language that was totally different from Japanese.

☼ **UNTIL THE SEVENTH CENTURY**, the Japanese had no way of writing their own language. During the Heian period, they looked to China in order to develop a writing system. By using Chinese characters, the Japanese were able to enrich their own language and record their ideas.

HANKO, or seals, were used as signatures. They were tubes of carved ivory or jade, with the character of the owner inscribed at one end. They were used by officials to sign important documents.

☼ **MAKE A HANKO**

You will need: orange paint, paper, felt-tip pen, sharp knife, potato

1 Ask an adult to cut the potato in half. Draw one of the characters on the right on the potato.

2 Ask an adult to help you cut around the character. Remove the unmarked bits of potato, so that the character stands out.

3 Paint the character and press it firmly onto a piece of ordinary paper, or special Japanese paper, to make a print.

▷ *These two characters read "Yamada," a fairly common name in Japan. Today, words of Chinese origin still make up more than half of all Japanese words.*

☼ **CALLIGRAPHY**, the art of handwriting, has been popular in Japan since the Heian period. At first, calligraphy was used to record Buddhist prayers and famous Chinese sayings and poems. The style and technique used to produce beautiful texts were greatly appreciated, in the same way that a painting might be admired. Special brushes were dipped in black ink, and a poem, or another piece of writing, was copied onto delicately colored sheets of paper. The way the words looked on the paper was just as important as what they said.

◁ *This girl is using calligraphy brushes to write a letter.*

FOR MANY CENTURIES, scholars and officials used the Chinese language for writing. However, the Japanese language, when spoken, sounded very different from Chinese, and Chinese characters were complicated and took a long time to write. A new system of writing was needed to record Japanese sounds and to simplify Chinese characters. A set of syllables called *kana,* which were originally based on Chinese, gradually evolved. Each *kana* syllable could be used to represent a Japanese sound. Over time, two sets of *kana* came into being, one called *hiragana,* and the other called *katakana,* and so, along with Chinese characters, there were three ways of writing. Sometimes, all three can be found within one sentence.

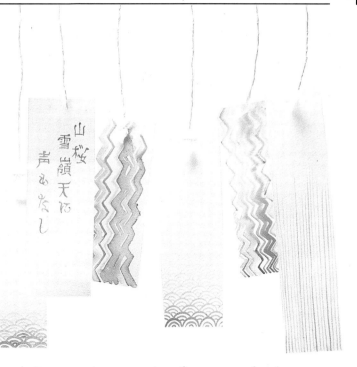

△ *Prayers written on strips of paper are often hung around Shinto shrines for good luck.*

yama

da

BY THE END OF THE 17TH CENTURY, many people were able to enjoy reading plays, stories, and poetry. This was due to more advanced methods of printing and people being able to borrow books from libraries.

JAPANESE LITERATURE began to emerge shortly after the writing system was introduced. The earliest recorded piece of writing is called *The Kojiki,* which means "record of ancient matters." It describes the birth of Emperor Jimmu and how the Japanese islands were created.

The first Japanese poems date from the end of the eighth century. The *Man'yoshu* is a collection of about 4,500 poems divided into 20 books. One of the themes running through the poems is a warning that life is very short and soon over.

木 = tree

山 = mountain

川 = river

田 = rice field

人 = person

口 = mouth

△ *Chinese characters developed from simple drawings. Gradually the drawings developed and became the characters that are used today.*

Arts and Crafts

Although China was a major influence on arts and crafts in Japan, the Japanese created their own sense of style. They made many beautiful paintings and **ceramics** that reflected Japanese history and culture. It was also important that even everyday objects, although simple, were beautiful.

☼ **THE ART OF PAPERMAKING** arrived in Japan from Korea in the seventh century. The Japanese soon found many ways to put paper to good use. Not only was it used as a writing material, but its lightness and strength made it a practical, and often beautiful, building material. It was also used for religious purposes, for writing prayers and marking sacred places with prayers written on paper strips.

☼ **PAPERMAKING**

You will need: wood strips, drawing pins, hammer, muslin, hacksaw, baking tray, food blender, nails, strips of white paper, flower petals, grass, cloths, glue

1 Ask an adult to cut four 7″ lengths of wood, and four 9″ lengths.

2 Glue or carefully nail the pieces of wood together to make two rectangular frames the same size.

3 Stretch a piece of muslin over one of the frames and pin it to the edge of the fame.

4 To make the pulp, tear the paper into small squares and soak in water overnight. Later, add more water and liquidize in blender.

5 For color, add some shredded flower petals and grass to the pulp.

△ *This 17th-century hand-painted screen is made of paper.*

🐸 **DURING THE EDO PERIOD,** the wives of fishermen and farmers made work clothes out of paper. They used a special type of paper, called *shifu*, that was made from twisted paper woven into strips. A finer version of *shifu* was also used to make tablecloths, handkerchiefs, and even mosquito netting.

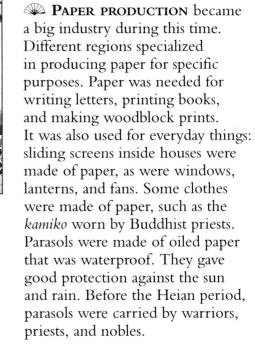

☼ **PAPER PRODUCTION** became a big industry during this time. Different regions specialized in producing paper for specific purposes. Paper was needed for writing letters, printing books, and making woodblock prints. It was also used for everyday things: sliding screens inside houses were made of paper, as were windows, lanterns, and fans. Some clothes were made of paper, such as the *kamiko* worn by Buddhist priests. Parasols were made of oiled paper that was waterproof. They gave good protection against the sun and rain. Before the Heian period, parasols were carried by warriors, priests, and nobles.

THE TEXTURE, COLOR, AND DESIGN of paper were all very important points to consider when writing a letter or creating a piece of calligraphy. During this period, paper designs became very intricate. Paper was dyed with blue, white, violet, indigo, and brown inks that were blended to form interesting shapes. Gold or silver patterns were sometimes printed on it, and even fine metal flakes were mixed into the paper.

THE PERSONALITY OF A WRITER was judged not only by the content of the letter, but also by the kind of paper he or she used. Therefore, anyone sending a letter would spend a long time carefully choosing the type and color of the paper and practicing calligraphy. Whoever received the letter could tell whether the writer had good taste or not.

6 Pour the pulp into the baking tray. Hold the frames together, with the muslin screen in the middle.

7 Dip the frames into the pulp, covering them completely. Take the frames out without tilting them. As the water drains into the tray, gently shake the frames from side to side, so that the pulp spreads evenly.

◁ *To make colored or patterned paper, add blades of grass, flower petals, or torn pieces of colored paper.*

8 To dry the paper, remove the frames, as shown above. Lay the muslin screen with the layer of pulp on it face down on a damp cloth. Use another cloth to mop up excess water on the muslin. The pulp should stick to the damp cloth; then you can gently peel the pulp and cloth away from the muslin screen.

9 Pin the cloth and layer of pulp up to dry or leave it in a dry place. When dry, lay the cloth face down and peel it away from the sheet of paper.

THE ART OF WRAPPING PRESENTS has always been very important in Japan. Before paper was commonly used, gifts were wrapped in fine cloth. There are still many special rules about how gifts should be wrapped; it is considered very poor taste not to wrap a present correctly.

LACQUER is a type of resin that comes from the lacquer tree, found in the northern parts of Japan. It was used on all kinds of objects, from tables to writing boxes, and vases to hair ornaments, to give them a hard, glossy appearance. Gold lacquerware was also used at banquets.

TO LACQUER AN OBJECT, it was first coated with lac, the sap collected from the lacquer tree. A piece of linen was placed on top of the layer of lac, and several more coats were brushed on. When the layers were dry, the surface was polished many times to give a shiny, black appearance.

MAKE A LACQUERED BENTO (LUNCH) BOX

You will need: scissors, thick cardboard, masking tape, glue, paints, varnish

1 Cut three squares from cardboard: base: 6³/₄", lid: 7", inside lid: 6¹/₂". For the side panels, cut eight rectangles: four measuring 6³/₄" x 2¹/₂" and four 6¹/₂" x 2¹/₂".

2 Glue matching side panels together for extra strength.

3 Tape all the pieces together, as shown above, to make a box. For the lid, glue the smaller square to the underside of the larger one.

4 Paint the outside of both the lid and the box black. Let dry.

5 Now paint the inside of the box and lid red, then let dry.

WOODBLOCKS were used for printing in Japan as long ago as the eighth century. The use of woodblock printing probably came from China and was first introduced by Buddhists, who used the blocks to print prayers and charms.

WOODBLOCK PRINTS in the 17th century showed the glamorous lives of *geisha*, actors, and sumo wrestlers. The world in which these famous people lived was so different from everyday life that it was called *ukiyo*, or "floating world."

MAKE A "WOODBLOCK" PRINT

You will need: craft knife, pencil, 4 polystyrene tiles, tracing paper, felt-tip pen, paint, paper, strong glue

1 Glue all four tiles together.

2 Draw the frog on the tracing paper. Place the tracing on the tiles. Go over the tracing with a pencil to leave an impression on the tiles. Go over the impression with a felt-tip.

3 Ask an adult to help you cut out the frog using a craft knife. Cut through the top two layers of the tiles so that your design stands out in relief.

AT THE END OF THE HEIAN PERIOD, new techniques in lacquerware were created. In one particular technique, tiny pieces of real gold and silver were sprinkled on to the lacquer while it was still wet.

6 Use gold paint to decorate the box. When the paint is dry, varnish the box to give it a laquered look.

AN ARTIST, ENGRAVER, AND PRINTER were needed to make woodblock prints. The artist made the original drawing, an engraver carved the drawing into the wood, and the printer applied the inks to the blocks and printed the image on paper.

4 Paint the raised surfaces with different colored paints. While the paint is still wet, turn the tile over and press it on to the paper to make a print.

DURING THE 17TH CENTURY, trade in porcelain and lacquerware became very important between Japan and Europe. Thousands of bowls, chests, and objects of art coated in lacquer or decorated with mother-of-pearl or ivory were shipped to Europe.

LACQUERED WRITING BOXES, decorated with mother-of-pearl or gold, were highly prized possessions for the Heian nobility. But, by the Edo period, these objects of art belonged not just to the privileged nobles and samurai. Ordinary people, who had perhaps become wealthy through trade, also wanted to buy beautiful objects to keep in their homes. Many people started to buy woodblock prints, and because they were almost as cheap as a bowl of noodles, it meant that most people could afford to buy a piece of art.

▽ *This woodblock print is copied from an 18th-century design called "Frog," by Matsumoto Hoji. You could use your hanko to sign your print.*

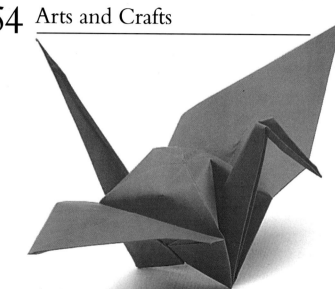

△ *An origami crane*

ORIGAMI, or paper folding, originated with the Shinto religion at the end of the Heian period. Figures of Shinto gods were made from paper and hung around shrines. It is thought that the first piece of origami was made by Fujiwara no Kiyosuke, a man who folded paper into the shape of a frog.

IN THE KAMAKURA PERIOD, nobles would attach a piece of origami to their swords to bring them luck in battle. Later, in the Muromachi period, special schools were opened to teach people the art of origami. As paper became more readily available, the art of paper-folding became a popular pastime for many ordinary people.

ORIGAMI FLAPPING BIRD

a	*b*	*c*	*d*	*e*	*f*

You will need: square piece of paper

1 Fold the paper in half along the two diagonals. Unfold, turn the paper over, and fold in half horizontally, then vertically. Make the creases very sharp. Unfold the paper as in *a*.

2 Fold the paper in half horizontally.

3 Hold both sets of corners and push all four corners inward as in *b*, to make a star shape.

4 Lay flat in a square shape, *c*, with the opening at the bottom.

5 Fold the edges of the top layer in toward the center crease, *d*.

6 Fold the top triangle down over the two triangles at the front, *e*.

7 Pull out the two folded triangles again, as in *f*.

8 Now, take hold of the bottom point and lift up the top layer of paper. Pull it up and back as in *g*.

△ *This porcelain dish was made in the town of Arita where the first Japanese porcelain was made.*

POTTERY was used in Japan as early as 800–300 B.C. Early pottery was made of clay that was shaped into basic pots for storing food. In the 16th century, Korean potters who came to Japan changed the style of Japanese ceramics. They set up kilns on the island of Kyushu and helped to create styles that later influenced the production of porcelain in Arita.

FROM THE 16TH CENTURY, tea bowls that were designed for use in the tea ceremony were considered valuable possessions. Some bowls were made to look old. A famous teacher of the tea ceremony, Sen no Rikyu, asked a tile maker to design a simple tea bowl. He made a plain bowl, such as a peasant might use. This simple style of pottery became known as *raku*.

IKEBANA, or flower arranging, has its roots in both the Shinto and Buddhist religions, where flowers were presented as offerings to gods. In the 15th century, a style of *ikebana* called *rikka* was introduced. Trees, shrubs, and flowers were arranged in a way that reflected a scene from the natural landscape. In the home, people used more simple arrangements with only one type of plant or flower. The longest flower represented heaven and the future, the second represented humans and the present, while the third represented the earth and the past.

▷ *Some flowers have special meanings: Japan's national flower is the chrysanthemum and represents the emperor.*

g   h   i   j   k   l   m

9 Pull the corner up and flatten out the diamond shape as in *h*.

10 Turn the whole shape over, *i*.

11 Repeat steps five to nine on this side. This will give you a long thin diamond shape with a smaller triangle hidden in the middle, *j*.

11 Fold the bottom triangles up and outward, below the center crease, *k*.

12 Fold the triangles back down. Open the sides of the diamond, and tuck the triangles up into the middle as in *l*.

13 For the head, turn the tip of one of the triangles over as in *m*.

14 Pull the upper parts of the triangle apart and fold downward to form the wings.

15 Hold the flaps underneath your bird and pull them gently back and forth.

MANY DIFFERENT SHAPES AND STYLES can be made in origami, from simple cubes to animals such as monkeys or rabbits. A very popular shape to make is the crane, which is the symbol of long life and good fortune. When people wish for something special, they sometimes fold hundreds, or even thousands, of cranes and thread them on long lengths of string. Then they hang the cranes outside Shinto shrines as offerings to the spirits.

▷ *The most important aspect of origami is that the paper is always folded — it is never glued or cut. Some of the best designs are also the most simple.*

Nature's Laws

Different religious beliefs have existed side by side in Japan throughout history. Families were happy to combine them in their daily lives, depending on their needs. The Shinto religion was used for births and marriages. But for matters concerning death, for example, when remembering or praying for dead members of the family, people followed Buddhist teachings. Confucianism, which originally came from China, provided strict guidelines for behavior within society. It stressed, in particular, the importance of treating elders with respect.

△ *The entrances to sacred Shinto shrines were marked by tall, wooden gates called torii, which were sometimes painted red.*

SHINTO means "the way of the gods" and is the oldest form of religion in Japan. Shinto followers believe in the worship of spirits called **kami**. These spirits are thought to live in the sky, islands, waterfalls, mountains, and tall trees. Mount Fuji, the highest mountain in Japan, is believed to be sacred. Some animals are sacred because they are thought to be the messengers of the *kami*.

THE SHINTO RELIGION has no sacred scriptures or set of rules. It developed from a mixture of folk tales and legends from the earliest days of Japanese history. A respect for nature has always been very important in Shinto. People tried to keep the local *kami* happy with offerings of food and drink in order to ensure a successful harvest and to protect themselves from bad luck.

MAKE A SHINTO SHRINE

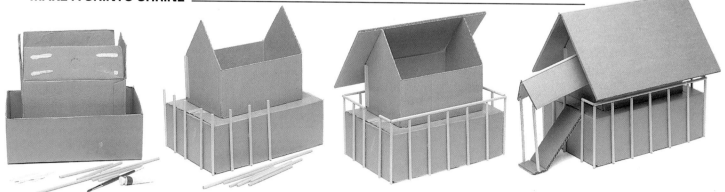

You will need: a large and a small cardboard box, thin doweling, four lollipop sticks, brown paint, masking tape, PVA glue, craft knife

1 Close the larger cardboard box and tape the lid. With the help of an adult, cut the smaller box into a house shape. Glue to the top of the larger box, as above. Carefully cut 20 lengths of dowel and glue around base of shrine as shown.

2 For the rail, carefully cut five long lengths of dowel to rest on top of the upright dowels. Leave a space for the stairs. Glue in place.

3 For the roof, ask an adult to help you cut two large sections of cardboard and glue them in place.

4 Cut a length of dowel the same length as the roof and glue along the ridge of the roof.

5 To make the stairs, carefully cut a long strip of cardboard. Glue at an angle to the first floor, as shown above.

6 For the porch, cut two cardboard rectangles. Glue together to form a roof shape. Fix two upright lengths of dowel to the base of the stairs. Glue the roof to the top of the posts, and shrine wall. Add a length of dowel along the ridge of the porch.

THROUGHOUT MOST OF THE HEIAN PERIOD, Shinto was the main religion practiced, particularly in the countryside and at the Heian court. People were very superstitious; anything to do with death, illness, or blood was to be avoided at all costs. If someone fell ill or died, bits of willow wood were hung from houses as a warning to keep away.

THE SHINTO SHRINES AT ISE are the most sacred shrines in Japan and date back to the fourth or fifth century. Until the 15th century they were visited only by members of the imperial family, but later they became a popular place of pilgrimage for many Japanese. One of the shrines is dedicated to the sun goddess Amaterasu. According to Shinto belief, the rulers of Japan are supposed to be descended from this goddess.

DURING THE EDO PERIOD, pilgrimages to famous shrines and temples became very popular. Some people saw them as a good excuse to travel with friends. Others went on pilgrimages to ask for special favors or to thank the *kami* if their family had received good fortune.

△ *Daikoku, on the left, is a Shinto god of luck. He carries a mallet for grinding rice and is associated with the rice harvest. Inari (the fox), on the right, is one of the most popular kami in Japan today. The red cloth is a sign that the kami is being taken care of. People make offerings of food and drink to the kami to keep them happy.*

7 To make the roof decoration, cut two lollipop sticks in half and glue into cross shapes. Glue a cross to the front and back of the roof ridge. Glue three short pieces of dowel across the middle of the ridge as shown above. Paint your shrine brown.

BUDDHISM is a religion that spread to Japan from China and Korea in the sixth century. It began in India with the teachings of Buddha, a man who lived from 563 to 483 B.C. He achieved **enlightenment**, a perfect mental and physical state, and spent the rest of his life teaching his disciples.

▷ *As Buddhism spread throughout Japan, many new temples were built with pagodas. Underneath the pagoda, relics of Buddha, such as pieces of clothing that he may have worn, were buried.*

△ *The Great Buddha at Kamakura was built in 1252. The statue is made of bronze and stands 38 feet high.*

upper stories used to view surrounding area

most Japanese pagodas are made of wood

DURING THE SIXTH CENTURY, Prince Shotoku encouraged the growth of Buddhism in Japan. The rulers of Japan were attracted to Buddhism because they thought that the whole country would be protected from danger if they followed this religion. Many temples were built throughout the country so that monks and nuns could study and teach.

IN THE HEIAN PERIOD, BUDDHISM became increasingly popular. The nobles at court found the complex beliefs even more challenging than Shinto. By the late 12th century, Buddhism had reached ordinary people. They were comforted by the belief that anyone could reach paradise by calling out to the Buddha to save them.

ZEN BUDDHISM was introduced to Japan in the late 12th and 13th centuries by a monk called Eisai, who had studied in China. Zen had some very strict practices. Monks would **meditate** for many hours, sometimes receiving sharp blows with sticks to help them concentrate more fully. It was also believed that you could meditate while doing normal jobs such as cleaning or even eating.

✗ **THE STRICT DISCIPLINE** that was needed to follow Zen Buddhism made the religion popular among the samurai. They were attracted by the calmness of the religion, the strict meditation routines, and the possibility of enlightenment. The samurai used many of these ideas to help them become fearless fighters, unafraid of death.

Zen ideas also had a strong influence on art and culture. In times of unrest, artists and scholars took refuge in temples and monasteries. As a result, Zen arts, such as gardening, calligraphy, ink painting, and the tea ceremony, flourished in these centers.

✗ ▽ **THE TEA CEREMONY** was practiced by Zen monks who drank tea to help them stay alert when they meditated. To help them concentrate, it was important to pay attention to every detail of tea-making, from boiling the water to the way the tea master whisked the green frothy tea in the tea bowl. The atmosphere was very quiet so that people could relax, meditate, and forget their normal lives. The same ideas also lay behind the design of a Zen garden.

△ *Water is incorporated into many Zen gardens to suggest a waterfall, ocean, or a fast-flowing river. Or else it may simply provide a soothing sound as it drips into a stone basin.*

✗ ▽ **ZEN GARDENS** were designed with Zen beliefs in mind. Sometimes water or flowers were used, or dry landscapes were created using moss, stones, gravel, and sand. Often the gravel was carefully raked into swirling patterns. An onlooker was supposed to imagine what all the different shapes in the garden might be. For example, rocks might represent mountains, or raked gravel could be a whirlpool or waves on the sea or a river.

✗ MAKE A ZEN GARDEN

4 Add the stones and moss to complete your miniature Zen garden.

You will need: cardboard box, thin doweling, plastic comb, small rocks, moss (from a florist's shop), sand, craft knife, glue

1 Cut down the sides of the cardboard box to make a shallow tray, as above.

2 Ask an adult to cut a section of comb. Glue the comb to one end of the dowel. Pour a layer of sand in the tray and shake gently until smooth.

3 Rake curved patterns in the sand, as above.

Japan in the Modern Age

Japan is now home to over 123 million people, which is the seventh largest population in the world. Most of the country is mountainous, so flatter areas are very densely populated. Japanese cities today have a modern feel to them, with skyscrapers and swift public transportation. As one of the most technologically advanced countries in the world, Japan has an enormous influence on world economy. However, tradition still plays an important role in Japanese society.

FESTIVALS are an important part of the Japanese year. People still gather to see the cherry blossoms and have picnics under the trees, just as the Heian nobles did. Carp streamers and dolls are put on display for Boys' Day in May and for the Doll Festival in March.

▽ *The tea ceremony is an important ritual in Japan today.*

△ *This park in Tokyo is crowded with people enjoying the cherry blossoms.*

TRADITIONAL JAPANESE ARTS are studied at special schools. Many women at some time or other study an ancient art, such as *ikebana* or the tea ceremony. Although most Japanese wear Western-style clothes, at weddings and other formal occasions they often swap their suits or jeans and T-shirts for kimonos.

OLD SKILLS often go hand in hand with new ones. At school, children learn subjects such as science and foreign languages, which will serve them in the modern age. The ancient skill of calligraphy is still vital, as young people have to learn to write up to 2,000 characters before they leave school.

△ *Inside a modern home in Kyoto*

AS USABLE LAND IS SCARCE, houses are often expensive and fairly small, especially in the cities. Some aspects of Japanese architecture have not changed since early times: a modern apartment may have one traditional Japanese room, with a *tokonoma,* *tatami,* and sliding paper doors. But the other rooms are more likely to be furnished in Western style.

△ *The Shinkansen, or bullet train, links Tokyo with Kyoto and Osaka, passing Mount Fuji on the way.*

JAPAN IS A LEADER in the manufacture of cars, rail technology, and in the electronics industry. Some Japanese companies are among the largest in the world, and many more are well known outside Japan. For over a century, Japan has been trading openly with other countries – mainly with its Asian neighbors, the United States, and Europe.

THE SAMURAI warrior has faded into history, but his legend lives on through comics, movies, and television. Although the samurai and shoguns no longer exist, Japan still has an emperor who lives in Tokyo, former name of Edo. He symbolizes the state and the unity of the people, although he has no real political power.

OVER THE LAST CENTURY, Japan has changed from being an isolated, inward-looking country to one that plays an active and successful part in today's world. Although it has adopted many modern practices and Western influences – from hamburgers to rock music – it has a strong cultural identity that is firmly rooted in its fascinating past.

▽ *Although many Japanese now play baseball and basketball, martial arts have gained in popularity – not only within Japan, but throughout the world.*

Glossary

The Ainu A group of people who once lived in northern Honshu and who now live in Hokkaido. They have a different appearance and culture from other Japanese people.

anthropology The study of the culture, language, origins, and behavior of people.

archaeology The study of the remains of buildings and artifacts left behind by people who lived in the past.

Buddhism A religion based on the teachings of Buddha (Gautama Siddhartha) in India in the sixth century B.C. Buddhists believe that they can reach a perfect state called enlightenment through meditation.

Bakufu The government set up by the samurai in the times when they had political control.

Bunraku A form of Japanese theater using puppets that are about half the size of a person.

calligraphy The art of fine handwriting. The characters are written from top to bottom and from right to left across Japanese paper. Sometimes the paper may be made by hand.

ceramics Objects made from pottery or porcelain. Japan is famous for its ceramic ware, such as *raku*, and some pieces are considered national treasures.

clan A large family group. For hundreds of years, Japan suffered from a series of clan wars, until single rule was imposed in 1603.

class structure The way in which people in some societies are ranked according to certain attributes, such as wealth or ability.

Confucianism A system of belief founded by Confucius (K'ung-fu-tzu) in China in the fifth century B.C. Confucianism encompasses a range of rules of behavior. These include being loyal to one's country and lord above one's family and obeying authority without question.

daimyo A powerful Japanese landowner who was also sometimes a military leader.

Edo period The period of Japanese history from 1600 to 1868, named after the city of Edo (Tokyo). It is also called the Tokugawa period.

enlightenment A perfect mental and physical state that Buddhists try to reach by meditating.

geisha A woman trained to entertain through music, dance, and witty conversation.

general election An occasion when the people of a country can vote to be represented in the government. They can choose from a selection of candidates of different political parties.

Go A game involving a board marked in a grid and two sets of counters. The object is to cover more space on the board with your counters than your opponent does.

hanko A cylindrical seal with a character carved at one end that is dipped in ink and used to "sign" documents.

Heian period The period of Japanese history from 790 to 1185, named after the city of Heian, which the Emperor Kammu made his capital.

historian A person who studies and writes about history.

ikebana The art of flower-arranging. It was originally part of Buddhist and Shinto rituals.

judo A martial art in which the contestants try to throw or wrestle each other to the ground.

Kabuki A form of Japanese theater in which actors in elaborate costumes and makeup perform using dramatic gestures.

Kamakura period The period of Japanese history from 1185 to 1333. It is named after the place in eastern Japan where the shogun Yoritomo established his military government.

kami Spirits that are worshiped in the Shinto religion. Kami can live in places, objects, animals, and people.

karate A martial art that involves fighting with the fists and feet.

ken A measurement used in house building. One *ken* is the length of a man lying down, that is, about 6 feet.

kendo A martial art in which opponents fight using bamboo staffs. Kendo developed from sword fighting and means "way of the sword."

kimono A loose-fitting garment tied with a sash that is traditionally worn by Japanese men and women.

lacquer A natural varnish from the lacquer tree used to harden and decorate objects.

martial arts Various kinds of armed and unarmed combat that developed in the East. Japanese forms, such as judo, karate, kendo, and sumo, developed from the fighting skills of the samurai warriors.

meditation Spending time thinking deeply and trying not to be influenced by things around you.

Muromachi and Momoyama period The period of Japanese history from 1392 to 1600. During this time, there were many wars between the different *daimyo*. Eventually, Japan was brought together under one ruler, Toyotomi Hideyoshi, in 1582.

Noh A form of Japanese theater that uses dance, mime, and masks.

origami The Japanese art of folding paper into interesting or beautiful shapes.

page A boy who becomes a member of a household in order to serve the master and to receive training in return.

political To do with the government of a country and its policy-making.

sake A type of wine made from rice.

samurai A Japanese warrior whose duty was to serve his lord, or *daimyo*. The samurai were the highest-ranking people in society.

shamisen A lutelike instrument that arrived in Japan in the 16th century. It is used in Bunraku and Kabuki theater.

Shinto A Japanese religion based on the worship of nature and the spirits of ancestors.

shogun The military rulers of Japan. From the 12th century until 1868, the shogun had more power over the country than the emperor.

shogunate The government established by the shogun.

society People living together in an ordered community.

soy sauce A sauce made from fermented soybeans and used to season food.

sumo A type of wrestling that originated as a harvest thanksgiving ritual in the Shinto religion. Sumo is the oldest sport in Japan.

sushi A dish made of raw fish, or vegetables, and rice.

tofu A type of food made from soybean milk that sets into a curd.

vinegared rice A sweet, sticky rice used in making sushi. To make it, rice vinegar, sugar, and salt are mixed with warm cooked rice.

Zen Buddhism A form of Buddhism involving meditation and self-examination that came to Japan in the Kamakura period. Zen Buddhism is passed directly from teacher to pupil, rather than relying on religious writings.

Index